Springer Series on Couples and Health

Across a long life together most couples face at least one significant health challenge, and negotiate multiple life transitions that can impact on their health. The central theme of this book series is that the couple relationship is a central influence on health, both physical and mental health. Partner interactions are so crucial that, in essence, couples conjointly cope with major stress. This conjoint coping can be positive and beneficial or negative and harmful.

There is now clear evidence that if health professionals work with couples, and help them conjointly to manage life stresses, it can meaningfully enhance health outcomes. The *Couples and Health* book series is intended to service the needs of professionals who work with couples, but who may not have expertise in working on health related issues. It guides professionals in the best evidence-based approaches to help couples better their relationships so that the relationship can become a buffer against stressful health and life events. This includes books focused on couples in which on spouse has a specific chronic health problem, and on books focused on couples making life transitions that are associated with health. While there is overlap among the books in terms of relationship enhancement material, each book provides unique health or event content pertaining to each title.

This series is intended to assist busy clinicians incorporate into their clincial practice the best available evidence on working with couples working within difficult circumstances. We hope you will regularly turn to the books in the series on your e-reader or book shelf when planning a client session and find useful information. If that happens then we have achieved what we set out to do.

W. Kim Halford and Tamara G. Sher
Series Co-editors

More information about this series at http://www.springer.com/series/11191

W. Kim Halford • Jemima Petch • Debra Creedy

Clinical Guide to Helping New Parents

The Couple CARE for Parents Program

Springer

W. Kim Halford
The University of Queensland
St. Lucia, QLD, Australia

Jemima Petch
Relationships Australia
Brisbane, QLD, Australia

Debra Creedy
Griffith University
Gold Coast, QLD, Australia

Springer Series on Couples and Health
ISBN 978-1-4939-1612-2 ISBN 978-1-4939-1613-9 (eBook)
DOI 10.1007/978-1-4939-1613-9

Library of Congress Control Number: 2015933614

Springer New York Heidelberg Dordrecht London

Printed on acid-free paper

Springer Science+Business Media LLC New York is part of Springer Science+Business Media (www.springer.com)

I dedicate this book to my wonderful wife Barbara, who made the transition to parenthood with me all those years ago, and with whom I made the transition to grandparenthood as this book was being written.

WKH.

To my husband and two beautiful boys. Together we have shared thousands of joyful moments—smiles and laughter I will never forget.

JP.

Parenthood can be hard but also a joy. To my husband Mark and my children Ben, Alison and Joe—you have made me stronger, better, and more fulfilled than I could have ever imagined.

DKC.

Preface

In this book, we present an evidence-based approach to relationship and infant care education for couples having a child together. The program is called Couple CARE for Parents (CPP), and is intended to assist couples to sustain and strengthen their relationship as they become parents.

CCP is distinctive from couple therapy. CCP is focused on relationship enhancement, relationship commitment, and prevention of relationship distress. CCP uses the positive feelings of the partners as a resource to build momentum for positive change as they adapt to parenthood. CCP also includes education and skill building to assist partners to support each other, and parent their baby in a sensitive and responsive manner. In contrast, couple therapy is focused on the treatment of existing relationship distress. Couple therapy necessarily deals with resolving longstanding grievances, negative thoughts, and feelings about the relationship.

CCP is most commonly provided in a mixed delivery format. In the antenatal period, which is when we recommend starting CCP, we offer couples a one-day face-to-face workshop. We find couples often appreciate the chance to share experiences with other expectant couples. Subsequent to that workshop we usually offer CCP as a mixture of home visits and flexible delivery. Flexible delivery is built around self-directed learning materials (such as online materials, printed worksheets, and instructional DVDs) that couples complete at home, usually with telephone-based or Internet-based support from a health professional. The home visit and flexible delivery are intended to make CCP easy to access. At the same time, different contexts and health delivery systems might make other program delivery formats more appropriate. This book describes CCP in the usual format in which we deliver it, but also describes how different formats can be used to provide CCP to couples.

This book has eight chapters. The first chapter briefly analyzes the most relevant research on what influences couple adjustment as they become parents, and what approaches to couple relationship education are most effective to assist new parents. Chapters 2–8 describe the units that make up CPP. There are descriptions of content areas to be covered, and specific couple and group exercises are presented. The book includes suggestions about how the content and process of CCP can be tailored to meet unique couple needs.

We aim to make the book useful to practitioners. There are boxed sections called Practice Tips that provide very specific suggestion on how to enhance the effectiveness of sessions with couples. We also have all the clinical handouts included in the book available as handouts that can be downloaded from the Springer link web site for this book at http://link.springer.com/book/10.1007/978-1-4939-1613-9. The effective delivery of the program also draws upon the personal experience and knowledge of you the reader. In order to prompt thinking on how your personal experiences might be used in delivering CPP, we have included boxed sections called Clinical Connections. In these boxes, we pose questions that we plan to stimulate reflection on how your personal experiences might be drawn on in program delivery. We hope that our writing captures the blend of applied science and compassionate practice that we think characterizes good couple relationship education.

St. Lucia, QLD, Australia W. Kim Halford
Brisbane, QLD, Australia Jemima Petch
Gold Coast, QLD, Australia Debra K. Creedy

Acknowledgements

We are very grateful to Dr. Jenny Gamble, who is a valued colleague and worked with us in conducting the large randomized control trial of Couple Care for Parents. Jenny has invaluable experience and wisdom in perinatal care, and her contributions to the training and supervision of our nurse-midwife educators in that trial were of great importance to fine-tuning the program. We also thank Joanne Fisher, Teresa Walsh, Corinne Mawn, Leesa Cunningham, Melinda Bentley, Jacqui Hudson, Alison Brennan, Lianne Schwartz, and Di Tamariki for their work as the nurse–midwife relationship educators in our research, their professionalism and skills helped to make the program effective. We also have a debt of thanks to Charles Farrugia, Vivian Jarrett, and Christopher Pepping for all their help with data collection on our research trials. Finally, we gratefully acknowledge the National Health and Medical Research Council of Australia grant 326321 "A randomized controlled trial of a couple-based program for the transition to parenthood" to W. Kim Halford and Debra Creedy that supported some of our research on Couple CARE for Parents.

Contents

Chapter 1
Couples Becoming Parents

Chapter Highlights

- Many couples struggle to adapt to parenthood and experience declines in relationship satisfaction.
- We can identify, to some extent, the couples who are at risk for struggling to adapt to parenthood.
- Brief couple education focused on adapting to parenthood can help.

Elaine slowly rocks her 6-week-old baby Jake. It is 3 am, and she has been up for more than an hour, feeding, changing, and trying to soothe him. It is the third night in a row that Jake has been difficult to settle after a nighttime feed. Elaine's husband Rob walks over sleepily and asks, "Can't you settle him? Have you tried feeding him?"

Elaine is irritated. "Of course I have, and changed him, and walked him around for an hour. Here Rob, you do something for once."

Rob: (Sighs) "What? I can't. After last night I have to get some sleep. I have to be at work early."

Elaine: "And like I don't get tired? Come on Rob, I'm exhausted."

As Rob and Elaine speak their voices rise in volume, and baby Jake escalates his crying. Elaine starts to cry and Rob retreats back to bed.

The vast majority of new born children live with their biological parents.[1] Parenthood brings an avalanche of change—some positive, some negative—to a

---

[1] Most of our work has been with heterosexual parent couples, but we believe almost all of the guidance in this book is potentially useful to Gay and Lesbian couples raising infants. A small but important proportion of new parents are not in a relationship with a partner. They also could benefit from assistance to adjust to parenthood. However, because single parents' needs are somewhat different from couples, we focus this book on the most common arrangement of a couple adjusting to parenthood.

W.K. Halford et al., *Clinical Guide to Helping New Parents*,
Springer Series on Couples and Health, DOI 10.1007/978-1-4939-1613-9_1

couple's life together. Parents watching their baby coo as he or she falls asleep, seeing their partner gently cuddle the baby they created together, walking together as a threesome—all can be wonderful experiences. At the same time, spouses struggling to wake in the middle of the night to yet more incessant crying, arguments with their partner triggered by exhaustion, and wondering if they will ever again have time together as a couple, can stress both partners. The stress can erode the quality of the couple's relationship. Infant care is often highly demanding and, like Elaine and Rob, many couples struggle to adapt to parenthood.

This book is a practical guide on how to educate and support couples to assist them adapt to parenthood. It is intended for psychologists, midwives, nurses, doctors, and other health professionals who work with couples becoming parents. The program presented is Couple CARE for Parents (CCP), which is a relatively brief (about 12 h of work for the couple across 4–5 months) structured program. CCP aims to help new parents develop shared and realistic expectations about parenthood, enhance their communication and mutual support skills, and promote sensitive and responsive parenting. CCP is built on adult learning principles so that each participant reflects on how they are managing the challenges and opportunities of becoming a parent, helps them develop self-change goals to enhance their adaptation to parenthood, and provides support to implement selected self-change goals.

This chapter provides a brief overview of the key changes in the couple relationship that result from the transition to parenthood. We also analyze the key risk and protective factors influencing couple and individual adjustment to parenthood, with a particular focus on the implications of this evidence for how best to support new parents. There is a brief review of the empirical evidence on the effectiveness of programs for assisting couples becoming parents. Finally we discuss the structure of CCP, and consider some practical issues in selecting how to offer CCP in different settings. The remaining seven chapters of the book focus on how to deliver each of the units that make up CCP.

Patterns of Relationship Formation and Dissolution

More than 85 % of adults marry at least once in their lifetime across most Western countries (Weston, Qu, & Hayes, 2012). A small, but increasing, proportion of the population choose not to get married, but most of them become involved in a committed couple relationship at least once in their lifetime (Australian Bureau of Statistics, 2012; Copen, Daniels, Vespa, & Mosher, 2012). These figures highlight the centrality of a committed couple relationship to almost all people's lives.

Cohabitation has some similarities with, but also some distinctions from, legal marriage. While almost all married couples report strong commitment to the relationship at the start of marriage (Weston et al., 2012), cohabiting couples differ widely in their reported level of relationship commitment (Rhoades, Stanley, & Markman, 2012). Some people cohabit after agreeing with their partner on a specific plan to marry. Other couples plan a future together that does not include marriage.

Yet other cohabitating couples have not discussed their relationship future with their partner (Hewitt & De Vaus, 2012). Even among cohabitating couples having a child together, there are couples who are unsure about whether they wish to be committed in the long term (Hewitt & De Vaus, 2012; Rhoades et al., 2012).

In most Western countries, such as Australia, New Zealand, United States (US), United Kingdom (UK), and Western European countries, there has been a modest decline in the rate of marriage across the last one to two decades, an increase in the proportion of couple households who are cohabiting rather than married, and elevated rates of divorce relative to 20 or 30 years ago (Weston et al., 2012). There also has been an increasing rate of cohabitating couples having children together, with 30 % of first-time parents cohabiting, rather than being married, in Australia and US (Australian Bureau of Statistics, 2012; Copen et al., 2012).

At the time of marriage or beginning cohabitation, people are typically optimistic about sustaining a satisfying relationship (Weston et al., 2012). However, the majority of couples experience some decline in their relationship satisfaction across time (Glenn, 1998; Halford, Lizzio, Wilson, & Occhipinti, 2007). About 40 % of Australian married couples (Australian Bureau of Statistics, 2012) and 50 % of US couples divorce (Copen et al., 2012). Rates of separation of cohabiting couples is not as well researched as rates of divorce, but estimates suggest rates of break-up of cohabiting couple is substantially higher than for married couples (e.g., Weston et al., 2012).

Clinical Connection
In what ways are cohabitation and marriage similar and different? How might you adjust the timing or content of relationship education for cohabiting couples as distinct from married couples?

The Couple Relationship and Parenthood

Most couples report that the birth of their first child is associated with feelings of joy and pleasure (Gottman & Notarius, 2000). Parenthood brings many rewards, including: (a) fulfillment of strong needs to reproduce; (b) fulfillment of social expectations; (c) a sense of achievement; (d) fun, affection, and companionship; and (e) is often seen as a symbol of love and stability in the couple relationship (Feeney, Hohaus, Noller, & Alexander, 2001). At the same time average relationship adjustment declines markedly across the first 1–2 years after the birth of a couple's first child. In a meta-analysis[2] of a large number of studies of couples becoming parents

---

[2] A meta-analysis is a way of combining statistically the results of multiple studies and it provides an estimate of the average effect across studies. Effect sizes are often classified as small, moderate, or large. (The statistical definition of effect sizes are: small is $d=0.3$ *SD*, moderate is 0.6 *SD*, and large is 0.8 *SD*.)

average relationship satisfaction was found to decline markedly in couples after having their first baby (Mitnick, Richard, & Smith Slep, 2009). Overall average relationship adjustment is substantially lower among parents of young infants than couples at other life stages (Twenge, Campbell, & Foster, 2003). While the average relationship satisfaction shows a decline, there is substantial variability around this average. About 40–50 % of couples show little or no decline, 30–40 % show a marked decline, and 10–20 % decline to the extent that they meet criteria for clinical levels of relationship distress (Petch, Halford, Creedy, & Gamble, 2012).

Infant Care

Many parents are surprised by the reality of caring for a newborn who is totally dependent upon them for food, warmth, and love (Vanzetti & Duck, 1996). Sleep disturbance, crying, and feeding problems are among the most commonly reported sources of stress for new parents. Newborn infants typically sleep for between 12 and 18 h, with the average hours of sleep declining gradually across the first few years of life (Galland, Taylor, Elder, & Herbison, 2012). Soon after birth, infants' sleep patterns are haphazard, with sleep occurring in relatively short bursts (up to 3–4 h) across the day and night (Teng, Bartle, Sadeh, & Mindell, 2012). When awakened, infants usually require feeding or parental soothing (Sadeh, 1996), and hence new parents frequently are caring for their infant through the day and night. Fatigue is almost universal among parents of infants (Sinai & Tikotzky, 2012), and extreme for approximately 30 % of parents who report sleep disturbances in their infants (Teng et al., 2012).

The clearest way infants can communicate their needs is through crying, and crying is most often used to communicate distress (Evanoo, 2007). The crying usually evokes a strong response in the parent(s), which serves to have the parent attend to his or her infant's needs, but if crying persists it can become very distressing to parents. Newborn infants most often cry when they are awakened, hungry, unsettled, too hot or cold, feel unwell, need a change in the environment (a reduction or an increase in stimulation), or need sleep (Barnard, 2010). Crying occurs on average 2 h a day (or more in the case of the 20 % of infants who are diagnosed with colic) up until the age of 3 months, after which time crying usually slowly reduces in duration (Barnard, 2010).

Breastfeeding is recommended for infants until at least 6 months of age, as it strengthens the immune system and enhances neuro-cognitive development (American Academy of Pediatrics, 2012). The parent–child interaction involved with breastfeeding also enhances infant attachment, especially when the mother enjoys the process of breastfeeding (Tharner et al., 2012). While more than 85 % of women can successfully breastfeed; the demands of breastfeeding for the mother are quite high. During the first 6 weeks of life, infants typically feed for up to 3 h per day with a recommended eight feeds spread throughout the 24-h day (Gettler & McKenna, 2011). Sustaining this frequency in breastfeeding can prove very challenging, especially for women returning to paid employment soon after the birth. Perhaps as a consequence only 60–70 % of women breastfeed at birth and only about 30 % breastfeed until 6 months (Blyth et al., 2002). Transient feeding problems are common and chronic feeding problems affect 25–35 % of infants (Manikam & Perman, 2000).

Impact of Parenthood on Parents

The experience of having a child is somewhat different for fathers and mothers. Partly this is due to the physical demands placed on women's bodies through the pregnancy, birth, and subsequent breastfeeding. The physiological changes associated with pregnancy, childbirth, and breastfeeding include hormonal variations, which can have a significant impact on the mother's psychological well-being (Clark, Skouteris, Wertheim, Paxton, & Milgrom, 2009). Often, the mother's experience during pregnancy (e.g., feeling the baby kick), makes the reality of becoming a parent more salient to her than the father. Similarly, experiencing the birth of the child for the mother often prompts a re-evaluation of her life situation (Clark et al., 2009). Many mothers experience mild depression (the blues) after the birth of their infant, and for some, these sad feelings persist and increase over time to a clinical level of postnatal depression (PND). Significant predictors of PND include prenatal depressed mood, high neuroticism, low social support, couple relationship distress, high rates of daily hassles or stressors, a history of sexual abuse, having an unplanned pregnancy, obstetric complications, perinatal stress, and a family history of psychological disorder (Klemetti, Kurinczuk, & Redshaw, 2011).

Postnatal anxiety disorders are also common in mothers, with an average of 3 % of mothers experiencing post-traumatic stress disorder (PTSD) after the birth of their child (Klemetti et al., 2011). Typically, women experience PTSD after having experienced complications during delivery such as severe injury, forceps delivery, difficult labor, or poor pain relief. Those mothers who experience pre-pregnancy psychological disorder (most commonly depression or anxiety) are at greater risk of experiencing depression or anxiety symptoms after the birth of their child (Teixeira, Figueredo, Conde, Pacheco, & Costa, 2009).

Although the majority of research has focused on mothers' psychological distress, a few studies have explored fathers' emotional health after the arrival of their infant. These studies have identified elevated rates of paternal depression and anxiety during the transition to parenthood, although the rates are not as high as in mothers (Schwalb, Schwald, & Lamb, 2013). The psychological distress experienced by mothers and fathers during the transition to parenthood places further stress on the couple and predicts increased risk of experiencing relationship distress (Schwalb et al., 2013).

There seems to be a reciprocal influence between individual psychological adjustment of the two partners and quality of the couple relationship. Rates of maternal reports of parenting stress, depression and worry are low when couple relationship satisfaction is high, and when women perceive their male partner as supportive (Florsheim et al., 2003; Wicki, 1999). If maternal depression does develop, recovery is predicted by being in a satisfying and supportive couple relationship (Pope, Evans, McLean, & Michael, 1998). Conversely, maternal depression predicts deteriorating relationship adjustment (Belsky & Kelly, 1994).

Impact of Parenthood on Couple Interaction

Along with infant care demands, there are at least five other major changes that new parenthood brings, which can contribute to deteriorating couple relationship satisfaction. First, there is often inequity in the division of infant care between mothers and fathers, which can be a source of dissatisfaction to women. The care of an infant adds approximately 35+ hours of work per week to the average couple household (Craig & Bittman, 2005). Many, although not all couples, report an egalitarian approach to housework before parenthood that they plan to maintain and expect to continue while raising their child (Katz-Wise, Priess, & Hyde, 2010). However, on average women, regardless of whether they are in paid employment, do about two to three times more of the extra work generated by having a child than men (Hansson & Ahlborg, 2012). The inequitable burden of child care responsibility can be a source of significant dissatisfaction to women, particularly if they expected and desired an egalitarian division of labor (Feeney et al., 2001).

Second, after the birth there is less time for couple-focused communication free from distraction. Relative to before children, on average after becoming parents couples' communication is characterized by the use of less self-disclosure, less praise, and increased negativity and conflict (Belsky & Kelly, 1994; Gottman & Notarius, 2000). Deterioration in couple communication is not as evident in couples who show higher than average positivity before the birth (Houts, Barnett-walker, Paley, & Cox, 2008), suggesting the stresses of parenthood exacerbate pre-existing difficulties in couple communication.

Most couples report stress associated with a decline in disposable income after the birth of their first child (Thomas & Sawhill, 2005). This decline is associated with both increased costs associated with having a child, and with a decline in income if the woman reduces her hours of paid work. Men often report an increased sense of responsibility to provide financially, and tend to increase their commitment to paid employment after the birth of their child (Astone, Dariotis, Sonenstein, Pleck, & Hynes, 2010). Particularly for couples on modest incomes, the financial squeeze can substantially erode their opportunities for individual and shared leisure activities (Thomas & Sawhill, 2005).

Fourth, there is reduced frequency and quality of couple time. During the last trimester and after the arrival of the baby, parents' social and recreational activities decrease, in particular their leisure time such as weekends away and holidays away from home (Claxton & Perry-Jenkins, 2008). When couples do manage to sustain shared activities with their partners they report higher relationship satisfaction and less conflict a year after the birth of their child (Claxton & Perry-Jenkins, 2008).

Finally, many couples stop having sex in the third trimester of pregnancy and do not start again until 2–3 months after the birth of their child (Johnson, 2011). Many new mothers experience discomfort or pain during sex before and/or after the birth of their child, which reduces the sexual activity of the couple (Sagiv-Reiss, Birnbaum, & Safir, 2012). In addition, many mothers, and some fathers, report reduced sexual desire attributable to a combination of fatigue and a reduced sense of sexual attractiveness in the woman (Hipp, Kane Low, & van Anders, 2012; Johnson, 2011). For some fathers the decreased sexual interest of their partner leads to frustration, especially if these men view sexuality as a key way to experience intimacy and for validating their partner's emotional closeness to them (Perini, Ditzen, Hengartner, & Ehlert, 2012). For about 30 % of new parents, sexual problems persist for at least 3–4 years after birth (Johnson, 2011; Sagiv-Reiss et al., 2012).

Couple Interaction and Parenting

The couple relationship is well recognized as a key determinant of the quality of family life and parenting of young children (Erel & Burman, 1995). Meta-analyses of the couple dyad and parent–child dyad indicate a consistent, moderate to large effect size relationship between good couple relationship functioning and sensitive parent–child interactions (Erel & Burman, 1995; Krishnakumar & Buehler, 2000).

Consistent with research findings on the association of the couple relationship with parenting of children, chronic couple conflict predicts low sensitivity and responsiveness of parenting of infants in the first year of life (Owen & Cox, 1997). This association is particularly strong when the infant is exposed directly to couple conflict (Crockenberg, Leerkes, & Lekka, 2007). There are several pathways by which couple conflict might interfere with sensitive-responsive parenting of infants. First, the conflict distracts parents from attending to the infant, and increases parents' negative affect and physiological arousal in ways likely to interfere with higher order problem solving (Bradbury & Fincham, 1987). Difficulties with problem solving are likely to delay parents' response to the infant and reduce their sensitivity of that response. Secondly, couple conflict generates parental stress, which predicts more infant crying (Wurmser & Papousek, 2008). Infant crying is stressful to parents and predicts deteriorating relationship satisfaction (Meijer & van den Wittenboer, 2007). Thus, there is potentially an escalating cycle of negativity and upset between parents and between parents and the infant. Third, low relationship satisfaction and high conflict is associated with disagreement between partners about sharing parenting and household responsibilities (Elliston, McHale, Talbot, Parmley, & Kuersten-Hogan, 2008). Such disagreements, in turn, predict deterioration in relationship satisfaction particularly for women (Feeney et al., 2001), and is likely to be associated with further escalation of couple conflict. Overall, the findings on couple relationship satisfaction, sensitive parenting of infants and maternal adjustment suggest mutual, reciprocal influences between these factors.

Clinical Connection
What are the more effective ways couples might address the common challenges associated with becoming parents? If you are a parent, how do you think you managed the transition to parenthood?

Risk and Protective Factors for Couple Relationships

The factors that predict couple relationship outcomes across the life span fall into four broad categories (Halford, 2011), which can be integrated into an ecological model that is depicted in Fig. 1.1. (1) At the outermost level of influence are socio-cultural variables, which provide the context in which relationships occur. There also are contextual variables that operate at a local level that differentially influence couples within a given culture. For example, positive support of the couple relationship by family and friends predicts sustained high relationship satisfaction (Larson & Holman, 1994). (2) Life events include major life events (e.g., birth of a child, a change of job) and daily uplifts and hassles (e.g., being praised by the boss, getting caught in traffic, and an argument with a co-worker). Stressful life events and daily hassles each predict deteriorating relationship satisfaction (Story & Bradbury, 2004). As depicted in the diagram, some life events are shared by the couple; other life events are experienced specifically by one partner. (3) Individual characteristics are relatively stable individual differences that partners bring to the relationship, such as negative family-of-origin experiences, low partner education, psychological disorder, and certain personality variables, each of which predict deteriorating relationship satisfaction (Bradbury & Karney, 2004; Holman, 2001). (4) Finally, couple interaction includes the partners' behaviors, thoughts, and feelings during interactions. For example, positive couple communication and shared realistic relationship expectations predict a sustained and mutually satisfying relationship.

The socio-cultural context in which the couple finds themselves plays a major role in how the relationship is viewed by the couple and by those with whom they interact (Halford, 2011). The couple's expectations, values, and beliefs are built upon the cultures they are raised and live in, and play a major role in the couple's ability to enhance and sustain their relationship. For example, couples with religious backgrounds tend to view marriage as important; couples that share this belief about marriage tend to stay together (Goddard, Marshall, Olson, & Dennis, 2012). Couples who come from very different cultural backgrounds sometimes integrate their differing expectations and draw on the strengths of those diverse cultures, while other couples struggle to reconcile their different expectations (Goddard et al., 2012; Halford, 2011).

A second aspect of context is the couple's life events. The transition to parenthood is one of the most significant changes a couple experience, and this can be made more challenging if the couple is experiencing other major change at the same

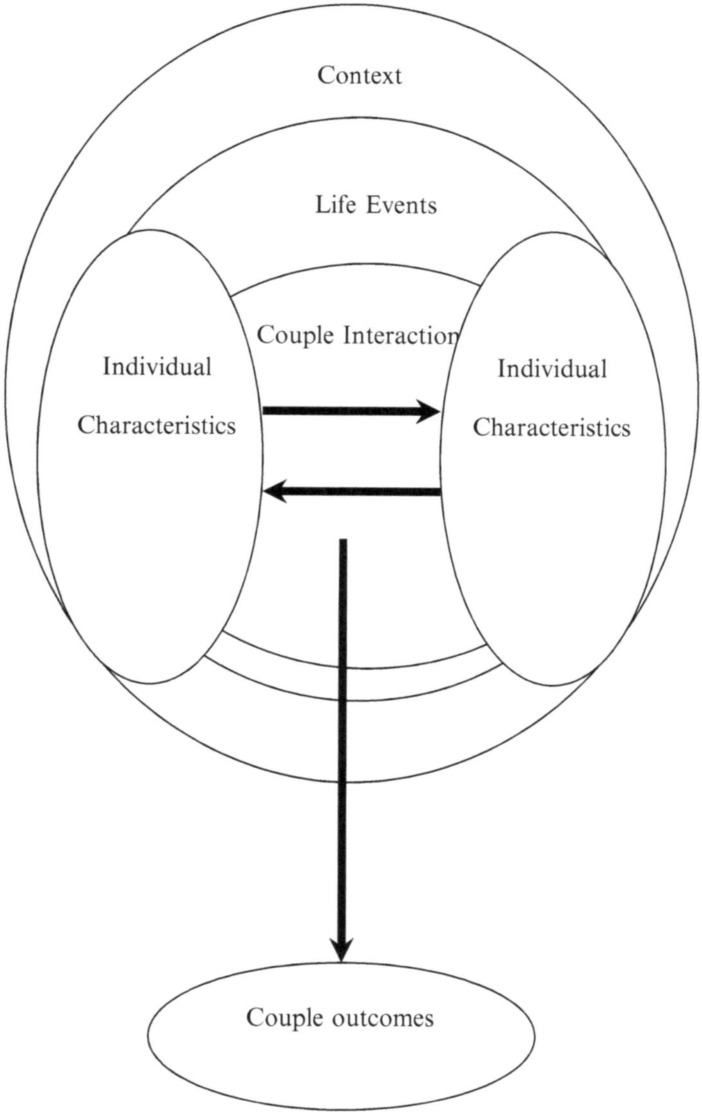

Fig. 1.1 An ecological model of influences on couple relationships

time (Neff & Karney, 2004; Story & Bradbury, 2004). Couples who transition to parenthood often need to accommodate their personal activities to those of increased household duties and care of the infant. These adjustments are associated with a decrease in quality time previously shared with their partner (Cowan & Cowan, 1992). Those couples who sustain positive communication and mutual support tend to develop a joint approach to coping with stressful events, which makes them resilient to the negative effects of life stress (Bodenmann & Cina, 2006).

With respect to individuals' characteristics, normal personality variations do not account for much of the variability in couples' relationship satisfaction, although emotional stability (low neuroticism) and high agreeableness are reliably associated with higher satisfaction (Dyrenforth, Kahsy, Donnellan, & Lucas, 2010). However, low relationship satisfaction is strongly associated with the presence of psychological disorders (e.g., depression, alcohol abuse, and some anxiety disorders, especially panic disorder and generalized anxiety disorder) in one or both spouses (Whisman, 2007). There also are some individual vulnerabilities that likely increase the risk of both individual psychological disorder and couple relationship distress. For example, individuals who show deficits in interpersonal communication and negative affect regulation are at elevated risk of developing both alcohol abuse and relationship problems, which in turn might exacerbate each other (Halford, 2011).

The couple's family-of-origin experiences also predict their relationship satisfaction (Halford, Sanders, & Behrens, 2001). In particular, spouses whose parents divorced or were violent toward each other in their family-of-origin are at risk to experience inter-partner violence, declining relationship satisfaction across time, and relationship separation (Halford, Sanders, & Behrens, 2000; Perren, Von Wyl, Bürgin, Simoni, & Von Klitzing, 2005). The long-term effects of negative family-of-origin experiences seem to be mediated, at least in part, by the communication skills individuals learn while growing up. Individuals who experienced parental divorce or inter-partner violence in their family of origin show more negative communication in the early stages of their adult relationships (Halford et al., 2000; Sanders, Halford, & Behrens, 1999), which likely reflect being exposed to models of negative communication by their parents. Negative communication mediates the association of family-of-origin divorce with declining relationship satisfaction across time in newlywed couples (Story, Karney, Lawrence, & Bradbury, 2004).

Lastly, how spouses act toward each other, and how they think and feel during those interactions, plays a significant role on couple relationship satisfaction (Halford, 2011). Specifically, couples who communicate positively, support each other, and manage conflict effectively tend to have more satisfying relationships (Halford, 2011). In addition, couples who self-regulate their relationship behavior (i.e., monitor their own behavior, set self-change goals, and change their behavior to enhance the relationship) report sustained relationship satisfaction (Halford et al., 2007). In contrast, couples who do not work on their relationship tend to blame relationship difficulties on their partner and report declining relationship satisfaction (Halford et al., 2007). In the case of expectant couples, those couples who discuss and plan the pregnancy adjust better to parenthood than couples who have an unplanned pregnancy (Bouchard, Boudreau, & Hebert, 2006). Shared and realistic expectations of the relationship, and how the couple will share the tasks of parenthood, predict sustained high relationship satisfaction in the year after the birth (Feeney et al., 2001; O'Brien & Peyton, 2002).

A couple's level of commitment to each other and their relationship also predicts relationship satisfaction (Iafrate, Bertoni, Margola, Cigoli, & Acitelli, 2012; Smith, Heaven, & Ciarrochi, 2008). Couples who view their life as a shared experience are more satisfied after becoming parents (Smith et al., 2008). Using dyadic coping (where both partners share their thoughts and feelings about stresses and seek to jointly manage the effects of stress) also predicts sustained high relationship satisfaction (Bodenmann & Cina, 2006).

Practice Tip
Research shows a complex array of factors (context, individual characteristics, life events, and couple interaction) affect couples' adjustment to parenthood. Individuals often attribute their adjustment to just one variable (e.g., "I am just not cut out to be a good parent."). Supportive education that highlights the broader influences can help people find ways to improve their adjustment (e.g., seeking additional support from others, talking differently to your spouse, and reducing stress by cutting back on paid employment).

Assessing Risk in Couples

The ecological model integrates the couple's socio-cultural context, life events, individual characteristics, and couple interaction in predicting relationship satisfaction across the transition to parenthood. In combination the ecological model allows prediction of which couples are at high risk for having difficulties adjusting to parenthood. By assessing that risk it is possible for professionals to ensure they provide high levels of support to high-risk couples. At the same time it is important to recognize that the assessment of risk is unlikely to ever predict future relationship satisfaction perfectly. Things that happen after the birth, such as having a sick or disabled child, and changing life events (e.g. loss of employment in one or both parents), are often not known before the birth and can profoundly affect couples' adjustment and need for support.

In brief, risk can be defined as those factors from the ecological model that predict declining relationship satisfaction. Specifically, as identified previously, financial stress, experience of parental divorce in the family of origin, inter-partner violence, and unplanned pregnancy are all established risk factors for poor adjustment to parenthood. In one study a count of the occurrence of these factors was used as an index of risk that could range from zero to six. High-risk scores were found to predict lower relationship satisfaction 2 years after the child was born (Petch et al., 2012). Taking a score of 3 or more as indicating high risk, it was found 45 % of high-risk couples became clinically distressed 2 years after the birth compared to only 20 % of low-risk couples.

Effectiveness of Couple Education for New Parents

There have been a large number of trials evaluating couple relationship education (RE) to assist couples becoming parents. A meta-analysis of 21 of these studies reported small effects on couple communication and relationship satisfaction

(Pinquart & Teubert, 2010). Many of the programs evaluated in these studies were very brief (one or two sessions), and these brief programs had little or no effect. Programs that were only offered after the birth of the child seemed to have, at best, small effects.[3] Moderate to large effect sizes occurred for interventions with five or more sessions held across both the antenatal and postnatal period. A limitation of much of this research was lack of long-term follow-up to evaluate whether there were sustained benefits of RE for new parents.

There have been seven randomized trials of RE for new parent couples that have assessed the effects of education for 12 months or more. Of these trials four found clear and substantial benefit of couple education, one had unclear findings, and two found no benefits of education. The first of the studies that found no clear benefit of RE was conducted with 290 couples who were recruited through a public maternity ward located in the Netherlands (Trillingsgaard, Baucom, Heyman, & Elklit, 2012). Couples were allocated to one of three conditions: the Positive Relationship Education Program (PREP), an information-based control group (INFO), or care as usual. Across 2 years, all three groups declined in relationship satisfaction, and no significant differences were found between the conditions.

The Building Strong Families (BSF) project is a very large ($n=6{,}212$ couples) eight-site evaluation of several different RE programs for unmarried couples expecting a child together. Within a randomized controlled trial design at each site, at 15-month follow-up there was no overall effect of RE across sites on relationship satisfaction (Wood, McConnell, Moore, Clarkwest, & Hsueh, 2012). Attrition and low attendance was a substantial problem across most sites, but supplementary analyses showed that the outcome averaged across all sites for even the couples attending RE was not reliably better than for matched control couples. At one site (Baltimore) there was evidence that couples receiving RE were worse off than the control couples. A notable exception to the otherwise null results was observed at the Oklahoma City site, where an adaptation of PREP for new parents achieved high rates of attendance and enhanced couple relationship satisfaction in participants. Interestingly, the total duration of the RE at this site was substantially shorter than at the other sites, yet this was the only program with evidence of positive effects. In a recently released 3-year follow-up of the BSF, the benefits of RE in Oklahoma city on relationship satisfaction had attenuated. But the program continued to have an effect in reducing separations from 59 % of couples in the control condition to 51 % of couples who received RE (Wood, Moore, Clarkwest, Killewald, & Monahan, 2012).

Shapiro and Gottman (2005) did a small-scale trial of RE with 38 couples expecting their first child. The RE consisted of a couple-focused workshop, plus five home visits that provided information and skills training, which was compared to a waitlist

[3] In addition to providing an estimate of the average effect across multiple studies, meta-analysis also can be used to estimate statistically what characteristics of a program influence how much effect that program has.

control. The pattern of findings on relationship satisfaction was complex with some initial deterioration and then improvement in the relationship satisfaction of couples receiving RE. Given the modest sample size in that study, the replicability of the unpredicted[4] curvilinear relationship adjustment trajectory of the intervention is open to question.

Schulz, Cowan, and Cowan (2006) evaluated a RE program that consisted of 24 weekly 2-h group sessions that ran from the last months of pregnancy through to well after the birth. They found RE enhanced relationship satisfaction through to a 5-year follow-up, which is impressive. However, the program involved a lot of RE and hence would be expensive to deliver, and require a substantial commitment for participants.

Cowan, Cowan, Pruett, Pruett, and Wong (2009) recruited 289 couples who were expecting their first child, or who had a young child. The couples were predominantly low-income couples of Mexican or European ancestry. RE consisted of 16 weekly 2-h group sessions focused on parenting, couple communication, individual stress management, and social support, with a focus on promoting father's involvement with parenting. The couple RE was compared with a father-only group covering similar content; or a single information session (control). Both the couple and father-only conditions showed higher relationship satisfaction than the control, with the couple condition producing stronger effects than the father-only condition 18 months after RE.

Halford, Petch, and Creedy (2010) recruited 71 couples ($n=71$) expecting their first child who were randomly assigned to either: (a) Becoming a Parent (BAP), a maternal parenting education program; or (b) Couple CARE for Parents (CCP), a couple relationship and parenting education program. Relative to BAP, CCP reduced negative couple communication from pre- to post-intervention, and enhanced relationship satisfaction in women but not men to 1 year follow-up.

In summary, four of the six trials of RE just reviewed produced positive effects but two studies did not. There are several possible explanations for the mixed findings. One plausible explanation is the characteristics of the couples in the studies. Given that only 40–50 % of expectant couples report a substantial decline in relationship satisfaction across the transition to parenthood (Doss, Rhoades, Stanley, & Markman, 2009), the small average effect of RE (Pinquart & Teubert, 2010) might reflect that many couples adjust well to parenthood without RE. One study found that in marrying couples only those at high risk of future relationship problems benefited from RE (Halford et al., 2001). Perhaps the benefit of RE for expectant couples is also moderated by risk.

---

[4] The changes in satisfaction across time can be described statistically as a trajectory, and a curvilinear trajectory is when change begins in one direction and the rate or direction of change alters across time. (For example, if couples' satisfaction declines from pre-relationship education to post-relationship education but then starts to increase later.) Complex curvilinear change requires a lot of data points to estimate accurately, and hence this study with a small sample of couples and a complex pattern of findings needs to be interpreted cautiously.

Petch et al. (2012) evaluated the effectiveness of RE in 250 couples expecting their first child. The couples were assessed on risk and randomly assigned to Couple CARE for Parents (CCP), a couple relationship and co-parenting focused education program ($n=125$) or the Becoming a Parent Program (BAP), a mother-focused parenting program ($n=125$). Risk was associated with greater relationship and parenting adjustment problems. Relative to BAP, CCP women decreased their negative communication and showed a trend to report less parenting stress irrespective of risk level. High-risk women receiving CCP reported higher relationship satisfaction, and were less hostile and intrusive in their parenting, than high-risk women receiving BAP. There were no effects of CCP for men on relationship satisfaction. However, high-risk couples were much less likely to be distressed in their relationship if they received CCP.

In summary, the balance of evidence supports the effectiveness of RE in assisting new parent couples to adjust to parenthood. Couple CARE for Parents is the only program that has been replicated in two trials to enhance couple relationship satisfaction, although several other programs also have found positive effects. Benefits are likely to be greatest for high-risk couples.

The Structure of Couple CARE for Parents

Couple CARE for Parents (CCP) consists of six units, which are designed to address the needs of most couples who are becoming parents. In CCP it is emphasized that there is no one right way to have a great relationship, and each couple is assisted to define how they want to relate. This approach involves the couple being provided information, and undertaking experiential exercises, to clarify their beliefs about what constitutes a good relationship, and to develop shared and realistic expectations for their relationship and the sharing of parenthood. Couples also are assisted to develop their couple relationship and parenting skills, to self-evaluate their current behavior in the relationship, and to self-select personal changes intended to realize their shared view of their relationship. This self-change focus encourages each partner in the relationship to take active responsibility for sustaining and enhancing the relationship. CCP covers those areas identified in the research reviewed in this chapter as predicting future relationship satisfaction, and the components of effective relationship education.

Table 1.1 summarizes the content covered in the CCP. As is evident from the structure, the program extends from the last trimester of pregnancy through to 4–5 months after the birth of the child. As described above, the evidence suggests starting programs before the birth are more likely to produce benefits for couples. However, sometimes it might be difficult to recruit couples during the antenatal period. In these instances, program content needs to be modified to be appropriate for couples after the birth.

Table 1.1 Structure and Content of Couple Care for Parents program

	Weeks from birth	Unit content
1.	–6, group workshop	Expectations of parenting, couple communication (Chaps. 2 and 3)
2.	–4, home visit	Conflict management (Chap. 4)
3.	+3, home visit	Taking baby home: infant care, stress management (Chap. 5)
4.	+6, self-directed	Sharing infant care: mutual partner support, social support, shared positive couple activities (Chap. 6)
5.	+9, self-directed	Couple caring and sexuality (Chap. 7)
6.	+12, self-directed	Looking ahead: managing change, preventing problems, sustaining a relationship focus (Chap. 8)

Practical Issues in Offering Couple CARE for Parents

Modes of Delivering Couple CARE for Parents

In order to enhance accessibility of support for new parents, it is useful to consider what modes of delivery are attractive to couples. We encourage providers to offer CCP in a range of delivery modes, recognizing that different delivery modes are likely to appeal to different couples.

CCP can make use of different combinations of delivery modes to enhance accessibility and cost-effectiveness. As we typically deliver CCP, the six units are offered in a mix of face-to-face groups, home visits to a single couple and flexible delivery. A full-day face-to-face workshop is provided to groups of couples when the expectant mother is about 6–7 months pregnant. Many couples are keen to access relationship education at that time, and willing and able to set aside time to attend a full-day session. The group session allows couples to learn from other couples about the diversity of expectations and approaches couples take to sharing parenthood.

In our most common form of CCP delivery, couples complete the final pre-birth and all four post-birth units at home, avoiding the inconvenience of travel when in advanced pregnancy or when caring for a young infant. There are two home visits by a relationship educator, one in the last month before the birth and the second about a month after the birth of the child. The visits give the educator opportunity to observe the home environment, which provides information on how the couple is managing. For example, if the home is very untidy with few safe places for the infant to explore, then education and assistance can be provided to develop a safe and stimulating environment for the child. The last three units of CCP are done in flexible delivery mode and involve the couple completing structured exercises together, and having a telephone call with an educator. The flexible delivery is cheaper and easier to implement than the home visits, as it does not involve travel for the educator, and allows couples to complete the program in their own home and at times that suit them.

Regular (about monthly) completion of units provides most couples with reasonable time to complete the various tasks, while limiting the duration of time they are committing to working on the program. It also encourages the couple to establish a routine for completing units, such as setting aside a particular evening in 1 week per month. Finally, it allows the CCP educator to address issues with couples as they become most salient. For example, expectations about how parenting will be managed are discussed before the birth, and reviewed soon after the birth. Parental concerns about common infant care challenges, like feeding, crying and sleeping, are addressed soon after the baby is born. Concerns about sexuality are addressed a couple of months after the birth when many couples are seeking to recommence sexual activity.

When running CCP with groups of couples the ideas are introduced and couples do exercises in the sessions, and this process allows use of the group processes to enhance learning. The content of each unit can be covered in a 2-h group session. However, having couples with a newborn attend regular sessions can be challenging. Therefore this book focuses predominantly on delivery to one couple at a time, at least after the birth. We also suggest ways that procedures can be adapted for other modes of delivery.

CCP also can be delivered in face-to-face mode in monthly sessions with one couple. In this mode the couple completes one unit per month over about 6 months from the last trimester of pregnancy through to about 4 months after birth, which seems to work well. In working face-to-face with an individual couple it is possible to work through the same ideas and tasks as with the group delivery format.

When CCP is provided in flexible delivery mode, couples complete the program at home, and need access to the CCP materials. In this modality, the typical time commitment for couples for each unit is 60 min to do the individual and couple exercises, and 45 min for the telephone call with the educator. The flexible delivery mode allows the couple to negotiate whether they want to complete the program more quickly, or space out units over a more extended period. However, we find the approximately monthly occurrence of sessions seems to work well for most couples.

Clinical Connection
What form and timing of sessions might work best for the couples you are likely to work with? What structure might be easiest to deliver in your system?

Learning Processes in Couple CARE for Parents

A distinctive characteristic of CCP is that it offers an active, skill-focused approach to relationship education. This means the sessions focus on having couples try out new ways of relating, and having spouses talk to each other about their relationship. There is some didactic input from the educator, but face-to-face sessions are structured primarily around couple-based activities. These activities always lead toward partners defining changes they wish to implement in their relationship between sessions.

The learning processes in CCP incorporate key principles of adult learning, principles that facilitate self-directed learning. First, CCP is designed to reflect Kolb's (1984) Experiential Learning Cycle. Kolb's cycle has wide currency in adult education, and there is significant empirical support indicating that it does describe how people learn from experience (Lizzio & Wilson, 2004). Kolb describes the learning process as an iterative four-stage cycle: (1) a concrete experience followed by (2) observation and reflection, leading to (3) the formation of abstract concepts and generalizations, leading to (4) hypotheses to be tested and applied in future action, which in turn leads to new experiences. In essence, this means people often learn from experiences and reflections on those experiences. It is necessary to provide didactic input (e.g., lectures, demonstrations) to introduce abstract ideas (e.g., a model of good communication). However, experiences that prompt people to be reflective around issues related to the idea (e.g., seeing an example of poor communication and being asked to reflect on what makes it poor communication), often enhances receptiveness and understanding of the abstract idea. Furthermore, once the idea is introduced adults are unlikely to apply it without experiences that prompt them to apply and then reflect on the idea (e.g., communicate with their partner and then use the model to self-evaluate their own communication).

Clinical Connection
What is the best learning experience you had in the last few years? How was that learning experience structured?

The experiences in each CCP unit reflect Kolb's (1984) experiential learning cycle. Each unit in CCP begins with an experience to prompt reflection, followed by an input of ideas, and modeling of key relationship skills. The presentation is structured to prompt further reflection on the personal relevance of the ideas and skills. For example, in the group format the CCP unit on communication begins by eliciting comments from different couples about what constitutes good communication, and the importance of communication in a couple's relationship. Each couple is invited to reflect on the different ideas offered by other couples. This is followed by modeling of good communication, and description of a model of effective communication. Partners then talk together reflecting on the strengths and weaknesses of their communication. In face-to-face delivery (groups or individual couples) the educator can model the key relationship skills via a demonstration.

There are exercises in each unit of CCP through which couples can relate the ideas and skills introduced in the program to their relationship. The exercises are a mixture of partners working independently and together, with each person self-appraising their own behavior in relation to a particular relationship topic (e.g., communication, caring, and support); setting their own goals for a desired self-change with the aim of improving their relationship; developing realistic strategies for implementing and monitoring the change; and seeking feedback on the progress and effectiveness of their change efforts. The learning for each unit is completed with a written self-change plan that helps each partner to consolidate and apply their learning. The program provides a structure that combines individual reflection with opportunities for couples to progressively share, discuss, and negotiate ideas and behaviors as they work through the tasks in each unit. Thus, consistent with Kolb's learning cycle, the program is structured to give couples experiences, prompt reflection on those experiences, and promote self-directed change.

In group face-to-face delivery the exercises completed by the couple are complemented with group discussion. For example, in the first unit that is delivered when the woman is pregnant, couples are asked to reflect upon the time taken to care for a new born infant. Group discussion often focuses upon just how demanding the care schedule is, and different ways partners can support each other with this considerable work load. We often have each couple identify and discuss a couple they know who has adapted well to parenthood. (Some expectant parents do not know any other parents with young children, and just identifying that they have no examples to draw upon is useful in itself.) We ask the couples about what behaviors they notice in the parents that lead them to believe that couple are adapting well to parenthood. We then ask each couple to tell the group a key relationship behavior they have identified as characteristic of good adaptation to parenthood, and we write the behaviors each couple identified up on the board. When couples discuss what they think are the most important behaviors to manage the transition to parenthood well, this often highlights that there are some behaviors important to most couples, and some behaviors that are important to particular couples.

After couples have completed the exercises, the educator's role is to prompt and support couples through the program. In particular, the educator reviews the concepts introduced by the lectures or discussion in face-to-face mode, and the exercises completed by the couple. The educator focuses on promoting self-directed learning by shaping and modeling self-change skills. For example, in the second unit on communication the educator listens to a sample of the couple's communication and then asks each partner to self-appraise their own communication. These self-appraisals are shaped by the educator to ensure that each partner has developed realistic and concrete ideas about specific strengths and weaknesses, which can be used to generate self-change goals. It is important to note that self-directed learning does not mean there is no input from the educator, but rather that the educator helps the partners to clarify and define their learning goals.

Research in adult education shows that interaction with an educator is often vital to learning (Rourke & Anderson, 2002). Specifically, learners often report the need for such contact to sustain engagement with the programs of learning, and feel they need to receive meaningful feedback quickly in order to guide future performance. Even though CCP can be completed in large part by couples at home if they have access to the program materials, the program was not designed to be a self-help program for couples. It has not been evaluated for its efficacy without an educator, and for that reason the program materials are only made available to educators rather than couples.

Conclusion

In summary, there are as number of key implications of the research evidence for practice of couple education for new parents. First, the substantial demands of infant care often surprise couples, and can erode couple relationship satisfaction and individual mental health. Second, the ecological model is a useful way to summarize the diverse range of factors that influence couple adjustment to parenthood, and can help identify couples who might be at particular risk for poor adjustment to parenthood. Third, couple education that addresses the challenges of parenthood, and promotes mutual partner support can assist couples, and is likely to be of particular benefit to high-risk couples. Fourth, education that is of 10–12 h duration, which begins in the antenatal period and extends into the postnatal period, is easy for couples to access even when busy caring for a young infant, and encourages self-directed experiential learning, is most likely to be helpful. The remaining chapters of this book provide specific guidance on how to deliver the Couple CARE for Parents program, which incorporates these research-based principles.

Chapter 2
Expectations of Parenting

Chapter Highlights

This chapter describes how to do the following:

- Establish group rules and encourage participation.
- Help couples develop shared and realistic expectations about infant care, and share parenting responsibilities.
- Assist couples to identify and plan for their support needs after the birth.

This chapter describes some practical issues about how to structure the running of Couple CARE for Parents (CCP) in a group delivery format, which is what we recommend for the pre-birth units. This chapter also describes in detail how to provide the first unit of CCP, which helps the couple prepare for the major changes that will occur after the birth. The aim of these pre-birth activities is to help couples develop realistic and shared expectations of parenthood (e.g., infant care demands, gender roles, preferred parenting practices), and to identify what additional support might be helpful in the early phases of parenthood.

The content and activities of the first unit of CCP are summarized in Table 2.1. Typically, it takes about 2½ to 3 h to cover the content and activities. Usually we combine these activities with the activities on couple communication described in Chap. 3, and deliver the combined content described in Chaps. 2 and 3 to small groups of couples in a full-day workshop (5–6 h contact plus appropriate breaks).

Electronic Supplementary Material: The online version of this chapter (doi:10.1007/978-1-4939-1613-9_2) contains supplementary material, which is available to authorized users.

W.K. Halford et al., *Clinical Guide to Helping New Parents*,
Springer Series on Couples and Health, DOI 10.1007/978-1-4939-1613-9_2

Table 2.1 Content and activities for expectant parents

Topic and aim	Tasks	Example activity
Develop realistic expectations of infant care	Document infant care demands	24 h clock of infant care demands in a typical day
Clarify expectations	Explore how the couple wish to divide the tasks of newborn care	Who will do what?
	Educator provides information on likely infant care demands	Exploring infant care expectations
Support needs	Introduce concepts of emotional, problem solving, and practical support. Plan for additional support needs	Identifying support needs and potential support people

Practical Issues in Delivery of Couple CARE for Parents in Groups

There are four issues that you need to consider before starting to run a CCP group. The first is the number of couples to include in group sessions. This might be influenced by the rate of couples expressing interest in your program. We usually run group sessions for between four and six couples. Any less than four couples and it can be hard to develop an effective group process. To maintain active skill training and attention for each couple, which is central to the Couple CARE approach, about one educator to every four couples is desirable. Groups with more than six couples can be run effectively, but require more than one educator to be present. If you have more than one educator, having an educator of each gender present is an advantage.

A second consideration is the venue. You will need a large enough room to comfortably seat all the couples in movable seats, and to allow the couples to space themselves out from each other when they are doing couple exercises. The spacing provides some privacy, and prevents the noise of others from being too distracting. Arrangement of seats into a half circle is helpful, as it allows the participants to see and talk to each other, while being able to see and hear the educator(s) when they are at the front.

Equipment is a third consideration. Couples and the educator(s) will need to write. Providing clipboards for the participants allows them to complete written exercises without desks or tables acting as barriers to interaction. A whiteboard or flip chart is essential for the educator(s) and group members to write up comments and key points during the session. If the group is larger, with more than six couples, it can be very helpful to have a radio microphone (to allow moving around the group) and an amplifier for the educator(s), so they do not have to strain to project their voices in order to be heard. Women, who typically have softer voices than men, might want to use a microphone even in smaller groups.

The final issue is care for the women who are in an advanced stage of pregnancy. Fatigue can be a problem in the third trimester of pregnancy, a desire to urinate frequently is common, and sitting for long periods can be uncomfortable. You may find that some women will need to leave the room every hour, so discuss the best way for them to leave the room without distracting others. Provide comfortable, supportive chairs and perhaps suggest that couples may like to bring a cushion to class for extra back support for the woman. Finally, giving the group a short break at least every 90 min, and encouraging gentle movement during the breaks, can be helpful.

One other issue you might want to consider is how you will manage if a couple, or a partner, misses a session. You might want to offer the chance of an extra session for the couple (possibly with a fee attached) to catch up on the material that was missed. Alternatively, you might give the opportunity to make up a missed session with flexible delivery, and provide the couple with self-directed materials to allow them to complete the work in their own time.

Sending couples a letter (or email) ahead of the first session is useful. We send a letter that welcomes the couple to the program, and congratulates them on the decision to invest time in enhancing their parenting and relationship. The letter provides people with directions on how to get to the centre, with a map and clear directions for public transport and parking. In the letter couples are encouraged to arrive at least 10 min before the scheduled starting time. We indicate that the sessions will start promptly at the designated time, and we will complete the sessions at the specified time. Providing these key pieces of information can help get the first session off to a good start.

Clinical Connection
In order to make the Couple CARE for Parents program easy to access for couples, what venue, what time of the day, and what day of the week might work best? What things can you do before starting the program to ensure people will find the venue easily, and be comfortable when they arrive?

Beginning the First Group Session

Since this is the first time couples come into contact with the educator(s) and the other couples participating in Couple CARE for Parents, the impression the couples form will likely influence their commitment and engagement in the program. When a couple arrive we show them into the room, provide a pre-prepared name badge of their first name, make a point of introducing ourselves to each couple, and ask some questions of them to get them talking. We then introduce them to at least one other couple. We make a point of trying to start the first session on time. In order for the workshop to engage participants, the educators need to facilitate group interaction, and maintain a good balance between the didactic and experiential components of the workshop.

Ground Rules for Group Couple CARE for Parents

When conducting group sessions of Couple CARE for Parents it is helpful to establish some basic ground rules for group sessions, which maximize the advantages of that format. Table 2.2 lists some ground rules that are useful to review. There are

Table 2.2 Suggestions for group ground rules

Ground rule	Rationale
The session is about helping couples manage becoming parents, to help you decide how you wish to work together as a couple	Almost all expectant couples aspire to be great parents, and to have their couple relationship enriched by sharing raising their child. Only about half of all couples achieve this, many find the stresses of parenthood challenging and find their couple relationship deteriorates. Learning what you are doing that is helpful is important—so you keep doing it—and learning what you can change to make parenting and your relationship even better is good too
There is no one right way to parent or to have a great relationship as parents; each couple need to find their own way	It is important that differences in beliefs and values are respected both within a relationship and between couples
All sessions begin and end at the scheduled time; whether it is a group session, a home visit, or a telephone-based session. The educator makes sure everyone sticks to time. Please be ready to start 5 min early, so we can start promptly	This is fair to everyone and prevents wasted time
What is said in the sessions is confidential and is not to be repeated outside	People need to feel free to discuss issues in the sessions that are important to them
Respect is important to relationships. Listen to your partner and to other people; do not interrupt	Everyone needs to be able to state their opinion
Some aspects of a couple relationship are private, and the staff and group members should respect a couple's right not to talk about some aspects of their relationship	The educator needs to help each couple find a balance of sufficient self-disclosure to benefit from the program without feeling pressure to disclose what they regard as private
A balance of work and fun makes the sessions go well	It should be enjoyable, but also task focused
If you are having problems speak to the educator	Even if couples are assessed carefully before the group sessions, it is still possible for a couple to struggle with ideas or to uncover challenges in their relationship that are of concern

three guidelines that are really important to emphasize at the start of the first session, and you could introduce the ground rules with words like the following:

"*Welcome, it is great to see you all. Congratulations on taking a really important step, working together to be good parents, and to having the very best relationship you can. Great families don't just happen, partners need to nurture and care for their growing family. We are pleased to work with you to help you nurture your family and your relationship together.*

There are a few ground rules about how we run the group sessions that seem to make them work better for everybody. First, after years of running sessions we are confident that there is no one right way to raise a child or have a great couple relationship. These sessions are not about telling you what to do. The whole point of the Couple CARE for Parents is to help each of you define as a couple how you want to care for your child, and how you want your couple relationship to be as you parent together. Second, respect for the views and opinions of others – the partner and other group members – is really important. Let people finish what they are saying. Do not immediately disagree with someone. Instead, think about what has been said, and be open to new ways of doing things. Third, some bits of your relationship are private. Different couples will have different boundaries about what they want to discuss in a group like this. A lot of the work we do will involve you talking with your partner. We will invite you to discuss things with the rest of the group, but you should feel free to say: 'I would rather not talk about this to the group' – and that is fine."

Icebreakers

One goal early in the first group session is to help group members get to know each other a little, and to feel comfortable talking with each other. A common method of breaking the ice is to have people introduce themselves to the group. That works satisfactorily most of the time, though for people who are less comfortable in groups that can be a slightly daunting way to start. Table 2.3 describes three different possible icebreaker exercises that focus on couple relationships, but also provide a comfortable way for couples to talk together. Any of these exercises can be effective and you might like to experiment to find what works best for you with the couples you are working with.

Infant Care Demands

The content of the CCP program begins with an activity aimed at eliciting participants' understanding of the tasks of caring for a newborn, the time those tasks will take, and the frequency with which they will likely need to be done. The couples are then led into an activity which asks partners to rate how much of each infant care

Table 2.3 Possible icebreaker exercises for Couple CARE for Parents group

1.	Have the couples talk together in pairs of couples for 5 min, telling each other their names, how long they have been together, and one thing they really enjoy doing as a couple. Each couple then briefly introduces the couple with whom they spoke to the group
2.	Have the couples talk together in pairs of couples for 5 min, telling each other their names, and discussing where they plan to have the birth and why they chose that venue
3.	Have the couples talk together in pairs of couples for 5 min, telling each other their names, and each couple describes a couple they know who are parents, and what that couple says is the best thing about parenthood

Table 2.4 Infant care tasks: how long and how often they are typically needed to occur

Infant care tasks	Time it takes on average	How often it might occur
Breastfeeding	10–60 min, but typically around 30 min	Every 2–3 h; at least 8 in a 24 h period up until 6 weeks of age
Bathing	30–60 min	Once a day
Changing nappy	5–15 min	8–12 times a day
Infant sleep	16–20 h a day	Haphazardly, likely in 1–4 h blocks
Infant fussing/ irritability	Two or three times per day	Anything from a few minutes to an hour or more
Soothing baby to sleep	6–10 times per day	Anything from a few minutes to an hour or more
Attending to crying	Two or three times per day	Anything from a few minutes to an hour or more
Extra household chores as a parent		
Extra washing	A daily load (soaking, washing, drying, folding, and putting away)	1 h
All tasks in total		30–35 h a week

task they themselves will do versus what they hope or expect their partner will do. Partners are invited to share their infant care expectations with each other. It is often helpful to provide some psycho-education about infant care demands and to normalize couples' growing awareness of the demands of parenthood. The session then moves to the different types of support that new parents might want, and participants individually write down their current support needs during the pregnancy and future support needs they think they will have during the newborn period.

Couples who have shared and realistic expectations of the demands of infant care may better manage the stresses associated with parenthood. Even though there is a lot of information available about baby care, most parents report that they felt unprepared for the demands of a newborn baby who requires constant, 24-h care, and is totally dependent upon them. Table 2.4 presents the common infant care tasks, how often these tasks typically need to be done, and how long the tasks typically take.

The activity requires couples to map out the needs of a newborn across a typical day, which can be introduced with words along the following lines:

"*Many new parents report that they are surprised by the amount of time it takes to care for their new baby. In this activity we use a 24 hour clock diagram to help us identify the parenting tasks you will be doing in those first months of parenthood, and estimate the average amount of time that is needed for those parenting tasks. This will help you get a feel of a typical 24 hours in a new parent's life.*"

Practice Tip

Educators can write tasks on the whiteboard so all couples can see the diagram. Couples also can complete the 24 h clock face on paper which they can keep for future reference and discussion.

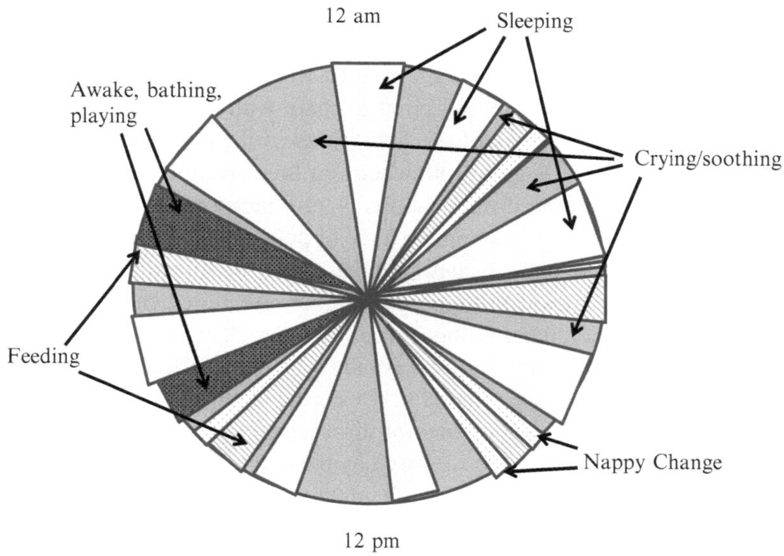

Fig. 2.1 24 h clock of infant care tasks

Couples use the 24 h clock diagram to write the task down according to the time of day it occurs and the amount of time it takes up. The 24 h clock is just a circle that can be divided off into sections as shown in Fig. 2.1. Figure 2.1 is an example of a completed 24 h clock. In a group workshop it is often useful to draw the blank 24 h clock on the whiteboard and then invite participants to start describing the infant care tasks, how long that task might take, and how often that task might need to be done in a 24 h period. When drawing tasks into the clock it is useful to ask participants when (i.e., what time of day) the task might occur and for the educator to draw the task into the clock like slices in the day so that participants gain an understanding of how the day might look like when caring for a newborn. This activity provides ample opportunity to provide psycho-education about infant needs and best-practices for parenting. It is important to emphasize that the clock is not a precise guide to how a baby will behave, but rather an opportunity to discuss the typical challenges of caring for a newborn baby. Asking participants to identify these tasks, time and frequency of the task, is key to engaging group members early on in CCP.

Practice Tip

As can be seen in Table 2.4 there is a wide range in the suggested times it takes to do tasks like soothing infant fussing, and attending to crying. These ranges are so wide because each child is different, and each parent attends and manages these demands differently. The educator should highlight that infants vary greatly in their behavior from one day to the next, and that some babies are much more demanding than others.

The 24 h clock activity often identifies misconceptions and unrealistic expectations about infant care. For example, many prospective parents are unaware of the frequency with which a newborn baby is breastfed and the length of time each breastfeed can take. Another helpful point to share with couples is that it is quite normal for a newborn to have four to six short feeds over 1 h in the first week of life. There are many potential negative influences on breastfeeding success, including worry about insufficient breast-milk supply, painful breasts (e.g., engorged, mastitis, cracked nipples) usually as a consequence of poor suckling attachment, as well as low support or negative views and attitudes about breastfeeding from partners, family, and friends. Women with supportive partners are more likely to successfully breastfeed and do so for longer. Without accurate and realistic information about the benefits of breastfeeding couples often have unrealistic or divergent expectations of breastfeeding, leading to disappointment, stress, and conflict.

Another example of the importance of discussing expectations relates to sleep and crying. Many new parents are surprised by the haphazard and broken pattern of sleep in newborns, and the extent to which infant crying can be a frequent source of distress to parents. Providing expectant parents with realistic expectations of normal newborn sleeping, crying and need for attention, helps each partner prepare and plan for the reality of infant care demands. It is also important to introduce the idea of sensitive and responsive parenting, which involves attending to infant needs in a timely and appropriate way. It is important to normalize that during the first few months of life almost all (95 %) infants cry when awakened, and that a timely parental response which assists the infant to return to sleep, or calm down, is considered sensitive and responsive parenting.

Sharing Parenting and Other Tasks

The 24 h clock activity helps couples clarify potential infant care challenges, and can usefully lead to discussion of how the partners will share the required tasks after the birth of their child. The educator can invite couples to complete the handout that appears as Table 2.5. This handout is designed to encourage couples to discuss ideas about who will do what infant care tasks and household chores in those first few months of parenthood. It is useful to have each partner independently complete the handout, and then to have each couple discuss their answers, identifying where they have similar and different expectations.

The activity of exploring the sharing of parenting and other household tasks can be introduced with an explanation something like the following. "*As a couple you probably have some patterns established around how you share household chores. I mean things like who does the cooking, the washing up, pays the bills, changes the bed sheets, shops for food, does household repairs, and mows the lawn. Having a baby adds to the tasks to be done, and it is important to have shared and realistic expectations about how all the work will be managed. This next activity lets you explore what your expectations are about who will do what in those first few months of parenthood. Please individually complete the hand out, and then we will ask you to discuss your answers with your partner.*"

Table 2.5 Who will do what? My expectations of housework and childcare
Think of when your baby is young (0–6 months old). Write what percentage of time you think you will do the task (0 = I will not be doing this, 50 = I will do this about half of the time it needs to be done, 100 = I will do this every time it needs to be done)

Task to be done	How much (0–100 %) of this task will you do?
Changing baby—wet nappy	
Changing baby—dirty nappy	
Feeding baby	
Sterilizing bottles/dummy	
Washing/sterilizing cloth nappies	
Bathing baby	
Dressing baby	
Attending to baby when she/he cries	
Holding/carrying baby	
Getting up to baby in the night	
Pushing the Pram	
Taking baby on outings	
Cooking—weekdays	
Cooking—weekends	
Shopping—food	
Shopping—baby items	
Washing dishes	
Tidying up around the house	
Vacuuming	
Laundry washing	
Ironing	
Washing floors	
Changing the bed sheets, towels, etc.	
Cleaning bathroom and toilet	
Cleaning kitchen	
Taking baby to doctor/hospital/child health	
Paying bills (e.g., electricity, telephone)	
Playgroups and mother/father groups	
Banking and financial planning/management	
Caring for pets	
Gardening	
Mowing lawn	
Repairs and maintenance	
Going to work/earning money to support family	
Other	

While many couples share household chores equitably in early stage relationships, it is common for new parent couples to become more traditional in their division of chores with the woman doing more of the household and child care tasks. This traditional division of labor might or might not be what each partner expected to happen. Women who expected a continuation of equitable sharing of roles can become highly dissatisfied with traditional gender roles. It is therefore worth exploring expectations with each couple. The educator's role in this activity is to support the couple to discuss any divergent expectations and facilitate the couple reaching a realistic, shared set of expectations (Table 2.5).

Practice Tip

It is worth drawing out in discussion four key points about the division of child care and household tasks.

1. Some couples share most tasks and each partner does about 50 % of the chores. This type of division of labor is reflective of egalitarian gender roles. Other couples have more traditional gender roles, in which the man goes to paid work while the woman stays at home (or goes to paid work part time). In traditional gender roles the woman does most of the child care and household chores.
2. There is no one correct way to share household chores but if partners disagree about the sharing of tasks, or see the sharing as unfair, this can create problems.
3. Many of our expectations about gender roles are learned when we are young and living with our parents. These expectations are sometimes not spoken about and sometimes we are not aware of them.
4. A common occurrence is for the woman to do a lot more of the child care and household chores than the man, even if both partners are employed full time. This arrangement is a common source of unhappiness for women.

Other expectations you may wish to explore with couples include the following. (1) What are the expectations about feeding the baby? For example, will the baby be breastfed and for how long? Will they feed their baby on demand or on a schedule? Who will do night feeds? When will they introduce a bottle, when will they introduce solids? (2) What are the expectations about sleeping? For example, will the baby sleep in a cot in the parents' room, or in a different room? Will they settle the baby to sleep, or let their baby cry to sleep? At what age will they expect baby to soothe him/herself to sleep? (3) How they will manage their baby crying? For example, will they always attend to the baby crying? What is the best way to attend to the crying? (4) What are their expectations about family and friends caring for their baby? For example, who will be allowed to hold the baby—young cousins? Who will babysit the baby—overnight, or on weekends? (5) Will the couple use day care? At what age? How often? Once partners have discussed a range of expectations it can be helpful to ask the couple to first summarize the expectations they agree on; second summarize the expectations they differ on, and how they differ on those expectations; and third, identify what expectations they will need to discuss further.

Support from Partner and Others

Many partners with a new baby benefit greatly from support they provide to each other, as well as support provided to the couple by extended family and friends. This next activity is intended to help couples anticipate what support they each might need as new parents, and plan how to access that support.

A useful way to introduce the idea of support needs is to discuss the type of support that people need in different situations. Table 2.6 is a useful handout describing different types of support. We ask couples to comment on what sort of support is needed (emotional, problem solving, practical, or information) and who might best provide such support for some common challenges faced by parents of new babies. Table 2.7 sets out some common challenges experienced by new parents that can serve as a useful basis for discussion. Table 2.8 is a handout that can be used to prompt spouses to discuss what sort of support they currently provide to each other, and how they might refine that support.

Sometimes this activity highlights key differences between partners in their views of who should provide what sort of support. For example, one partner might be keen to seek support from extended family while the other partner feels the

Table 2.6 Types of support
There are four types of support we can give to or receive from our partner

Emotion-focused support	
• Asking someone how their day has been • 100 % concentrated listening • Focusing on the positives about a person and praising their actions and effort • Attending to and encouraging the person's expressions • Validating your partner's feelings	• Helping your partner express their feelings and talk about an issue • Asking questions and paraphrasing someone's feelings • Offering affection with touch and hugs • Showing affection • Giving re-assurance
Problem solving support	
• Help someone define the problem • Summarizing and asking questions	• Suggesting options • Suggesting a specific plan of action
Practical support	
• Offering practical support like transport, garden care, shopping, etc. • Offering practical support in your partner's interests and hobbies • Regularly reviewing who does what and how much housework, childcare, and paid work in your relationship	• Offering practical support for household chores and house maintenance • Offering practical support in the tasks of parenting
Information support	
• Sharing information with your partner • Advice and guidance	• Asking for information and advice from professionals, friends, or family

Table 2.7 Common challenges of parenthood that might benefit from support

1. Kamala had her first baby 2 days ago and is finding breastfeeding difficult and very painful. Her mother had trouble breastfeeding and Kamala does not know if she will be the same as her mother. What sort of support might Kamala want in this situation? Who might best provide such support? How could you get that support if you were in this situation?
2. Roseanna and Erico have been taking turns to feed, burp, and re-settle their 3-month-old baby at night. Roseanna is on maternity leave and Erico is working. Erico feels so tired he cannot concentrate at work and almost fell asleep driving home one night. What support might Erico need in this situation? Who might best provide such support? How could you get that support if you were in this situation?
3. Bethany's 6-week-old baby has been crying on and off for a couple of hours most evenings when she is trying to cook dinner, eat dinner, and then clean the kitchen. Tonight she is home alone as her partner is working late and she feels she cannot stand the crying anymore. What sort of support might Bethany want in this situation? Who might best provide such support? How could you get that support if you were in this situation?
4. The demands of child care have surprised Yong and Ling Mei, and both are feeling exhausted. Preparing meals in the evening is proving a real challenge, and a couple of times recently they have eaten take away food, but they cannot really afford to keep doing that. What sort of support might they want in this situation? Who might best provide such support? How could you get that support if you were in this situation?

Table 2.8 Support needs: complete this individually

How does your partner support you at the moment? ....

....

What is an example of your partner giving you very helpful support................

....

Are there behaviors that your partner did recently that you have found unsupportive? If so, what were they? ....

What would you like instead? ....

How do you support your partner at the moment? ....

....

Parenthood

What support needs do you think you will have as a parent of a newborn baby?

....

How would you like your partner to support you as a new parent? ....

....

How will you ask for this support? ....

....

From who (other than your partner) will you seek support? ....

....

How will you support your partner as a parent? ....

....

As a couple discuss your support wants and needs and fill in the following table with your joint answers

The support we will need	Strategies for getting our support needs met
From each other	
From other people	

couple should be able to manage on their own. On average women are more likely than men to want a close relative (e.g., the child's maternal grandmother) to stay at their home for the first few weeks after the baby is born. Such a support person can provide invaluable support around baby care, meal preparation, and helping with some of the housework. Indeed, in many cultures it is expected that a woman's mother will come and stay for several weeks. It can be useful to highlight that the expectations people hold about involvement of grandparents, and other extended family, often varies across cultures and genders.

There is another common gender difference in support needs. In general, women particularly value emotional support. Women are more likely than men to seek emotional support for themselves, and to provide emotional support to others. The woman's focus is often on talking about experiences and feelings, with the idea that the talking itself is helpful. Men, on the other hand, tend to particularly value practical and problem solving support. Men are more likely than women to seek to generate solutions to problems when discussing stress. This gender difference can be highlighted by asking the men in the group a question like the following.

"*Gentleman, have you ever had your partner tell you about something that is worrying them about the pregnancy, like how the baby is kicking, how her back/hips/legs are aching, or that she is having trouble sleeping? Have you also found no matter what you suggest it seems to be the wrong thing?*" You might also pose the following question of women. "*Ladies, have you ever gone up to your partner to talk about how your pregnancy is going, how the baby is kicking, your back/hips/legs are aching, or you are having trouble sleeping. You really want to be listened to, but you feel he just keeps telling you what to do?*"

Many couples identify with this misunderstanding of what support is desired. Many women feel misunderstood and concerned that their man does not listen. Many men try to provide solutions, as they assume that is what their partner wants, and feel they cannot say the right thing. The activity suggested below allows partners to describe and discuss their support needs, allowing each partner to become more aware of what they can provide in order to support their partner. The activity can be introduced as follows.

"*This next activity gives each of you an opportunity to write down what type of support you want now and once you are a parent. I will then ask you to share your notes with each other and come up with a joint plan listing for getting the support you want as a new parent.*"

The educator should circulate around the room among the couples helping them to clarify their individual and shared support needs. Some useful questions to pose of partners in this process include the following. (a) What sort of support do you tend to give to your partner most often? (b) What sort of support do you think you will want as a new parent? (c) From whom can you ask for that support? (d) In those early weeks what sort of support will you want from your partner? (e) How will you ask for that support?

Completing the Group

As discussed earlier, we recommend offering both Units 1 and 2 (content addressed in the next chapter) as a single-day long workshop. After completing both units, the session can be drawn to a close by congratulating couples on completing Units 1 and 2 of CCP and providing a summary of the main points covered during the session. The remaining units of CCP follow a similar pattern, with a mixture of individual and couple activities. There will also be DVD resources or reading. In each unit, a self-directed change plan occurs, where each person puts into action what they have been thinking and talking about.

The educator may also ask participants if they have any questions, worries, or ideas from the workshop. Depending on time, these questions could be answered in the group, or followed-up in a telephone call at a convenient time.

Managing Common Challenges in Running This Unit

Disengaged Participants

The ground rules of CCP may help educators prevent disengagement or address it early when they see it. Help engage participants by making the CCP workshop and sessions interesting by: (a) using an engaging and varied tone of voice; (b) including anecdotes, real-life examples, and jokes (but check they are appropriate to the context and participants); (c) using a range of modalities and varying them: e.g., including activities that require some reading, some listening, some talking and some "live" practice of skills in group, couple, and individual activities. If just one or two participants are appearing disengaged you could use the participant's names when inviting them to share in a group activity, and ensure you talk to each participant during one-on-one activities to hear what their thoughts and comments.

> **Clinical Connection**
> Think back to a presentation that you recently really enjoyed. What made it enjoyable? What can you do to make the CCP sessions interesting, dynamic, and engaging for a variety of participants?

Couple Starts Arguing in Session

Chapters 3 and 4 introduce communication and conflict management skills and strategies to assist couples manage conflict. The ground rules at the beginning of CCP may also be helpful to review with the couple one-on-one if the couple conflict arises because the partners are interrupting each other, or immediately disagreeing with something the other partner has said. In this situation the educator might briefly join the couple, ask them to pause their conflict, reflect what is happening, and ask what each partner themselves could do to work through the activity with their partner. If they continue to struggle the educator could also suggest the couple complete the activity individually and write down what key messages they each want to communicate with their partner before speaking those messages aloud to their partner.

Couple Knows Very Little About Infant Care

Couples who know very little about infant care can be very vague about their expectations, or unrealistically optimistic about infant care demands. Psychoeducation about infant care (as in the 24 h clock activity) can assist individuals form more realistic expectations of the future needs of their own infant. Another possible strategy to help participants learn more about the variability of infant care and parenting is to ask them to talk to other new parents, read books, blogs or watch shows about what new parents do in a day of caring for their baby, how long things take and how parents manage those challenges.

Couple Has Very Different Expectations

In this first unit it is helpful to normalize that divergent expectations are common for many couples, and that neither partner is right or wrong. It is important that the educator help the partners talk to each other about where their expectations came from and then be open to identifying options for how they as a couple might proceed with finding a mutually agreeable solution.

An example of how an educator might work with this divergence in expectations and support needs is illustrated by Tom and Laura who were 8 months pregnant when attending the pre-birth unit of CCP.

Educator: So, we have been looking at what sort of support you may each want as new parents. What have you identified in your list of support wants?

Tom: I don't think a new baby has to change our life very much. We've talked about sharing the baby care and household chores – I do lots of the housework already anyway so I think we will be fine. I haven't put any new or extra support needs on my sheet.

Educator: Uh-huh, and what about you Laura?

Laura: I put heaps down!! (laughing). I really want my mum to stay for a few weeks after the baby is born, you know, to help me out with the baby, bathing, settling, and to help with dinner and some housework. I saw how much my friend struggled those first few weeks and she was always so exhausted. Plus, my midwife said the other day that if I could rest as much as possible in those first few weeks and take it easy then I would recover better after childbirth. So, I put down that I want instrumental support mostly, and I would like my mum to help give that to us.

Educator: I hear that you have different expectations about what support you want for those early weeks of parenthood. Have you had a chance to talk just now about how you will work through that difference?

Laura: I'm going to ask my mum anyway. I really want more support and I want to look after my body and rest. I know Tom doesn't get along so well with my mum but it will only be for a few weeks.

Educator: So, it sounds like you have a strategy to get the support you want Laura but that this strategy may not be Tom's ideal?

Tom: You're right there. I am going to feel uncomfortable with your mum there; do you mean she'll sleep over as well? I really think we will be right without her. You know I will do the dinners and stuff.

Laura: Yes, you do a lot around the house. I'm just worried though that I will need more help. Mum's had four kids and so will know a lot about what it is like, you know, if I have any breastfeeding problems, or just be there with me to figure out why the baby is crying, or what if the baby got a rash or sick? Mum would know what to do.

Educator: I can hear you have a variety of reasons why you would like your mum to stay. You've mentioned instrumental support, I wonder if you can, Tom, identify which other support needs Laura is listing?

Tom: I think she might be saying she wants her mum's emotional and problem solving support as well.

Educator: Uh-huh, I agree, does that sound right Laura?

Laura: Yes, I think I do want her there for all of the four different types of support. And it is not because I think you won't be doing enough, its more about me thinking I want nothing to go wrong in those first few weeks, I feel a bit anxious being alone those first few weeks especially when you are at work.

Educator: Okay, so I heard that you both have somewhat different expectations about what support will be useful in those early weeks. Laura would like her mum to stay because she feels her mum will be able to provide extra instrumental support, information, emotional support, and problem solving support. Tom however, feels more hesitant about his mother-in-law staying and thinks you two will be able to cope on your own. When I asked before if you had a chance to discuss how you will manage this difference in expectations I heard Laura that you wanted to ask you mum to stay anyway. How do you think Tom will feel if you chose that option?

Laura: Umm… he might feel left out, and he said he would feel uncomfortable. (turning to Tom) I don't want you to feel uncomfortable. What should we do? Maybe I could ask my mum to come only after you go back to work. Then you and I can do it all together in those first two weeks? Or, maybe I could try to have her over for only a few days each week? She would probably be okay with just a night or two, and then you and I can talk about if that is working? If I am coping…if you feel comfortable?

Tom: Yeah, I like that idea better. Especially about it just being the two of us for the first 2 weeks. I don't want you to get stressed out when I am back at work, so maybe we can try having your mum over for the third week and see how that works out.

In the above dialog, the educator assists the partners to clarify Laura's support needs and facilitates a discussion between the partners to identify a way forward that meets both of their needs. In exploring support needs, it can be useful to make the point that there is no one right way to be supported in the early months of parenthood. The expectations people have vary by culture, in some cultures it is normally expected the woman's mother or other relative will stay with the couple for an extended period after the birth of a child. Couples need to find the best way for them, based on shared and realistic expectations about how they will manage parenthood.

As noted previously, we most often run the content in the current chapter, and the content in the chapter that follows, as a single-day workshop. If the program is being run so the content of the current chapter stands alone it can be useful to ask couples at the end of the session what each of them found the most useful content that was covered, and if they have any further questions or concerns.

Chapter 3
Couple Communication

Chapter Highlights

This chapter describes how to do the following:

- Give the rationale for including couple communication in the program.
- Explain the intent–impact model, which outlines components of effective communication.
- Describe ten key communication skills and use them to guide participants to self-evaluate their own communication skills.
- Help partners develop self-change plans to enhance couple communication.

This chapter describes the second unit of the Couple CARE for Parents (CCP) program which focuses on communication. As noted in the previous chapter, we typically combine the content of Units 1 and 2 into a single one-day workshop provided before the birth. The aim of the current unit is to help couples practice and refine effective communication. The content and example activities are summarized in Table 3.1. The unit begins with the educator briefly presenting the intent–impact model of effective communication, and describing and demonstrating ten key communication skills. Each participant evaluates their communication by doing a communication task with their partner, and then self-rates their own individual communication skills. Each partner then writes a self-change plan that specifies a communication skill they want to improve.

Electronic Supplementary Material: The online version of this chapter (doi:10.1007/978-1-4939-1613-9_3) contains supplementary material, which is available to authorized users.

W.K. Halford et al., *Clinical Guide to Helping New Parents*,
Springer Series on Couples and Health, DOI 10.1007/978-1-4939-1613-9_3

Table 3.1 Content and activities for this chapter on communication and self-change

Topic and aim	Tasks	Handouts
Promote understanding of effective couple communication skills	Present a model of communication Present key communication skills	Fig. 3.1 Intent–impact model of communication Table 3.2 Ten key communication skills
Communication self-assessment	Practice and self-evaluate key communication skills	Table 3.3 Communication skills self-evaluation form
Communication feedback	Present guidelines for giving and receiving feedback Use feedback to enhance communication self-evaluation	Table 3.4 Guidelines for giving and receiving feedback Table 3.5 Less helpful and more helpful feedback examples
Communication self-change plan	Assist individuals chose a communication self-change plan to implement over the next week	Table 3.6 Self change plan Table 3.7 How to write a self-change plan Table 3.8 An example of a completed self-change plan

Communication

Communication is an aspect of couple relationships that partners rate as very important, and good communication is associated with high relationship satisfaction. Good communication includes: being actively engaged in a conversation with high levels of active listening, self-disclosure, and positive affect; while remaining calm and demonstrating low levels of hostility and criticism. In contrast, poor communication is characterized by high levels of negative affect (e.g., contempt, disgust, fear, hostility, emotional withdrawal), and negative reciprocity (e.g., increased likelihood of negative behavior following negative partner behavior).

Clinical Connection
How do you evaluate your own communication skills with an intimate partner? Do you feel confident that you can model good listening and speaking skills or do you need to work on your own communication to do such modeling well?

The communication skills covered in this chapter are used in later CCP units as well. For example, in Chap. 4 the communication skills are extended and applied to managing conflict in relationships. Chapter 7 includes use of communication skills applied to couples discussing the sensitive topic of sexual intimacy.

The material covered in this communication unit can be introduced along the lines of the following: "*Communicating well is one of the key things couples say makes them happy. Being able to talk with, and really feel understood, by your partner makes people feel loved and special. On the flip side, partners often feel sad or angry if they struggle to talk with each other, and feel misunderstood. Unhappy couples often say that they do not communicate well, and it is the most common problem people present in couple therapy.*"

Understanding Good Communication

It is useful to have couples consider what constitutes good communication. One good way to get them started is to pose the couple(s) the following question. "*I want you to think about a couple who you know well and believe communicates well. It can be your parents, or friends, but pick a couple in which you think the partners communicate well with each other. Talk with your partner about who you picked and tell them what you think is good about the couple's communication.*"

If you have a group of couples doing the above exercise, move around the group and listen to what people are saying. Help people to be as specific as possible about what behaviors they identify as good communication. For example, ask them what things someone does to be a good listener, or to be a good explainer of their ideas and feelings. When you hear a good example, ask the person if they will share that with the group once the couple discussion is done. Then you can ask particular people to share good ideas with the group at the end, and write these up on a whiteboard.

Practice Tip

If the group is struggling to be specific about good communication skills the educator can demonstrate poor and good listening skills. Ask someone in the group to speak with the educator briefly about a hobby or interest. The educator first listens poorly (e.g., not attending, looking away, being inactive) and asks the person to continue and then listens well (e.g., attending, asking questions, summarizing). The participants are asked to describe the differences between the two examples of listening. A similar demonstration can be made of clear, succinct speaking versus vague, lengthy and monotone speaking.

There are a number of helpful ways you can assist partners to focus on the behaviors of a good communicator. Questions like the following can help individuals understand more about communication behaviors: (a) what would you see a good communicator doing? (b) If you were to videorecord a good communicator and watch the recording what would we see? Remember to have people describe non-verbal behavior as well as the verbal content of good communication. You might also like to prompt people to attend to skills that make a good speaker (i.e., when people express their own ideas and feelings) and the skills that make a good listener.

Once participants have discussed their ideas about key communication behaviors with their partner, it is useful to review what they came up within the group. Writing the ideas up on a whiteboard can help to clarify and reinforce concepts. If you have cultural diversity within your group of couples you might like to ask different people how the rules of good communication might vary across cultures. For example, direct communication by saying exactly what you want or how you feel is often preferred in Western cultures. However, in many Eastern cultures the use of direct communication might be seen as rude.

Clinical Connection

Have you seen or been told of different communication rules for different cultures? The following quotes from people about how they think good communication works can illustrate how culture makes a difference. Mee Ling (Chinese woman married to a Western man) mimicking affectionate tones: "*I don't like 'honey, honey' ... 'love'. It's* [physical and verbal affection] *not important. Affection is when we work together. Let's say we need to prepare food for Chinese New Year – this is where the affection comes in.*"

Janet (Western woman married to Yang, a Chinese man): "*For me, communication is the key. It's vital that both partners are able to express their emotions, and there has to be an understanding response.*" Yang: "*She treats me like a rubbish bin to fill with her negative stuff. It's not right. I keep my negative feelings out of her sight.*"

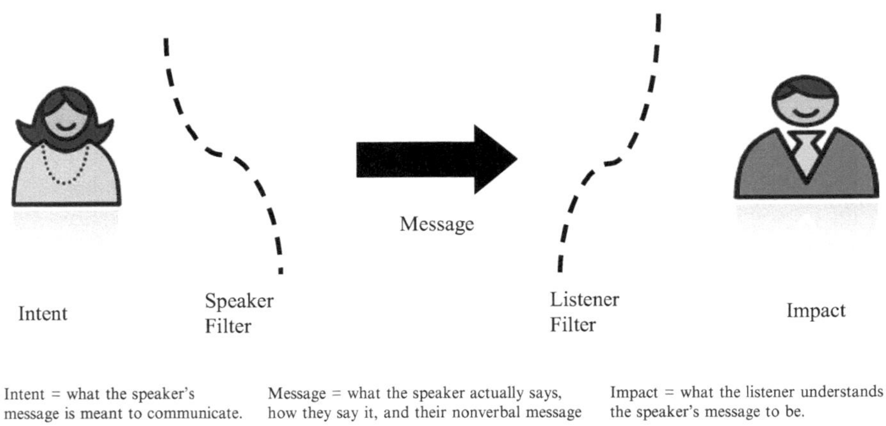

Fig. 3.1 Intent–impact model of communication

Once participants have identified good communication skills, including some listening and speaking skills, praise them for their efforts. It is useful to then show couples the intent–impact model of couple communication, illustrated in Fig. 3.1. This model can be given as a handout, or drawn on the whiteboard.

A useful way to introduce the model goes as follows: "*When we talk with each other we are continuously moving between two roles – the speaker and the listener. This is illustrated neatly with the intent–impact model. When the speaker has something to say they have an <u>intention.</u> The intention is the feeling, thought or idea that the speaker wants to express. The speaker then speaks. What the speaker says, how they say it, and how they look when they speak is the <u>message</u>. The message is what an outside observer can see and hear.*

Sometimes the intent equals the message and sometimes not. Have you ever said something and then realized it did not come out the way you meant it? When your message does not reflect your intent it is because of this filter (refer to filter on the left). A filter is anything that changes the message so it does not match what the speaker intended to say. Filters can be: mood, speech habits, and facial expressions.

The listener also has a filter (on the right). The listener's filter is anything that changes their understanding of the message. Examples of listener filters include the listener thinking he/she already knows what the speaker is going to say, not listening carefully to specific detail, listener being distracted by something else/some other thought, or the listener's mood. What the listener understands by the message is called the impact.

Clinical Connection
Think of an example of when you misunderstood your partner's or a friend's intended message. Can you think of what filter might have been a problem? Think of a time when your partner misunderstood you. What filter might have contributed to this misunderstanding? Could you use these examples to illustrate the ideas of intent, impact and filters to couples in Couple CARE for Parents?

Good communication occurs when intent = impact. Intent can be distorted by speaker filters or listener filters, so that the intent is not the same as the impact."

There are three general points to make about the intent–impact model. First, good communication is made up of both speaking and listening. Couples who communicate well share these roles, giving each person time to speak and to listen to each other. Second, filters can interfere with communication. If we have learned habits in the way we speak or listen that function to filter out intended messages, we can learn to recognize and remove those filters. For example, if we want to make a suggestion for change, but it often comes across as an order, we can learn to express things more gently. Third, there is no formula for "perfect" communication. Research shows that good communication varies by situation, culture, and topic. Hence in Couple CARE for Parents we do not prescribe particular ways to speak. Instead we ask each partner to reflect upon what is good about their speaking and listening, and what they might want to change.

Key Communication Skills

When couples struggle with their communication it can be useful to review their use of key effective speaker and listener skills. Effective use of the following key communication skills can help couples communicate with less potential for misunderstanding. In Couple CARE for Parents partners are shown a system of classifying communication skills into "speaker skills" and "listener skills." The intent is not to make couples use all of these skills, or only these skills, or only a combination of

Table 3.2 Ten key communication skills

Speaker skills	Listener skills
1. **Be specific**: Provide clear and concrete descriptions of behaviors or situations	5. **Attend**: Focus on your partner as they speak. Make eye contact, face your partner, remove distractions
2. **Express positives** (even if things seem mostly negative): Say positive aspects of a situation or your partner's behavior	6. **Listen actively** (even if you disagree): Say things like "Uh-huh", "Go on", "I see" so your partner knows you're interested
3. **Be considerate when expressing negatives**: Say what you dislike or want to change without being aggressive or rude	7. **Summarize content**: Put in your own words the key points of what your partner just said
4. **Self-disclose feelings**: share your thoughts and feelings with your partner	8. **Paraphrase feeling**: summarize your partner's emotion. (The emotion might be said in words, or communicated by how your partner talks or looks.)
	9. **Ask open questions**: Ask open questions that do not have a yes/no answer
	10. **Hear your partner out**: Let your partner finish speaking, do not interrupt, avoid immediately disagreeing. Put our opinion on hold until later

these skills, rather the intent is for couples to have a common understanding and a common label to describe particular speaker and listener skills.

When introducing speaker and listener skills it is helpful to provide couples with a handout that describes those skills (see Table 3.2). It is also important to demonstrate the skills. Some participants will have vague or inaccurate understanding of these skills. The goals of this unit are for participants to have a clear understanding of the skills, be able to demonstrate them, to evaluate their communication skill strengths and weaknesses, and then choose one skill to work on over the next week (as part of their self-change plan).

When describing a skill it is important to demonstrate that skill as well. An example introduction to this activity could be "*Let's review some key communication skills that research has identified as useful to help intent=impact. We've listed 10 skills – 4 speaker skills and 6 listener skills. Let's go through the definition of each, and demonstrate the skill as well. This will help us know that we are all thinking about the skills similarly. Practicing these ten skills helps improve couple's understanding of each other. It also improves openness and intimacy. Later in this chapter there is an activity in which you can assess your use of these specific skills.*"

Self-Evaluation of Communication Skills

Once couples have read through, discussed, and seen a demonstration of each skill, it is useful to get couples to practice using the skills in a conversation. If this is done in a group setting ask couples to disperse themselves around the room or in a few

Table 3.3 Communication skills self-evaluation form
Place a tick in the appropriate box to describe how you think you went during the discussion using this key
0 No use of this skill
1 Some use of this skill
2 OK, but could be better
3 Good use of this skill
N/A Skill not applicable

	Skill	0	1	2	3	N/A
Speaker skills	Be specifics					
	Express positives					
	Be considerate when expressing negatives					
	Self-disclose feelings					
Listener skills	Attend					
	Actively listen					
	Summarize content					
	Summarize feeling					
	Ask open questions					
	Let partner finish					

My communication strengths: ....
....
Things I need to work on in communication: ....
....

rooms nearby so they have some privacy. The exercise involves completing the following steps: (1) Each partner identifies a topic each to talk about. One good topic is to have each person describe an interest or hobby of their own that their partner does not know much about. Alternatively the person might describe something that is worrying them, or that they would like to change about themselves. It is preferable in this initial communication training to avoid discussing issues that are a source of conflict between the partners. (Conflict management is covered in the next unit of Couple Care for Parents.) (2) The couple decide who will be the speaker first and who will be the listener first. (3) The couple has the discussion with one partner staying in the speaker role, and on partner in the listener role for about 5 min. (4) The couple stop the discussion and each partner evaluates their *own* communication skills using criteria outlined in Table 3.3. (5) The partners swap roles (i.e., the partner who was speaker now becomes the listener and vice versa) and discuss the other topic for 5 min. (6) After stopping the discussion, each partner again evaluates their *own* communication using the same form. During the activity the educator needs to listen carefully to the conversation, making note of one or two strengths of each partner (i.e., the particular communication skills each partner is good at), and noting any excesses and deficits in use of particular communication behaviors. These impressions of the communication of each partner form the basis for the educator to guide participants' self-evaluation of their communication.

Practice Tip

When working with multiple couples in a group workshop it is important that an educator listens to at least 1–2 min of each couple's conversation. While listening it is useful for the educator to take some notes on each partner's strengths (skills they do well), excesses (what each person does too much of), and deficits (what each person might usefully do more of). These notes make it easier to remember the specifics of each couple's communication.

An example of these notes is the following:

Strengths: Mick (listener)—good attending, use of encouragers
Tahlia: (speaker)—clear description of the issue at the start

Excesses: Mick (listener)—used lots of closed questions
Tahlia (speaker)—described specifics, maybe too many details/facts

Deficits: Mick (listener)—minimal encouragers, silences, asking questions about feelings
Tahlia (speaker)—no self-disclosure of feeling

Because the educator plays an important role in helping partners identify their communication strengths and areas to work on, it is useful for the educator to pause the couple's conversation after a few minutes of listening and ask each partner some open-ended questions about the skills they are using. Facilitative questions educators could ask include: "*What skills are you noticing that you are using? What skill do you think was strength for you in this conversation? When you were talking with your partner now how similar or different were your speaker and listener skills to how they are when you usually talk to your partner? What are one or two skills you think you need to work on?*" The educator can help shape up partner's understanding of the skill and shape up accurate self-assessment. An example dialog of how an educator might facilitate such a discussion with a couple is provided below:

Educator (after listening to a couple for 1–2 min): "I'd like to ask you to pause there for a moment. Let's review how you each were going with the speaker and listener skills. Can you each take a couple of minutes to fill in your assessment sheet? (Pause) What skills did you notice you were using well Jill?"

Jill: "I was talking about how Scott and I should figure out where the baby will sleep, in our room or in the nursery. I've asked him before and feel like he hasn't really seen it as any big issue, but it is for me. I noticed myself being specific – like describing how he has seemed distracted and didn't really help me figure out the pros and cons of where we would all sleep better. I gave that skill a 3. And I noticed that I self-disclosed my feelings – I said that I was upset and annoyed at him and felt he wasn't really taking my concerns seriously. I gave that skill a 3"

Educator: "Uh-huh, you noticed two key speaker skills – being specific and self-disclosing your emotions and felt you did them well. It's great that you can describe your example of each skill. Was there a communication skill that you felt you could work on or do better?"

Jill: "Umm, I'm not sure."

Educator: "Ok, well let me check in with Scott and we can maybe return to areas for improvement. Scott what communication skill do you think was a strength for you in this conversation?"

Scott: "I was being the listener for most of this conversation and I think I was good at showing I was listening – you know, nodding my head and paying attention. The thing is that it was hard for me to do – I felt she was too negative and she dismissed solutions I offered".

Jill: "Yeh – I could tell you were getting annoyed at me"

Educator (gently interrupting): "OK, so I am hearing that Scott was using 'pay attention' as a listener skill. How did it feel for you Jill to have Scott really pay attention in this conversation?

Jill: That was really good. It made me feel like he was interested in what I had to say, and I talked about it more then I might otherwise have.

Educator: Great, so the things you did well in this talk included Jill: self-disclose feelings, describe specifics and Scott: pay attention. I also noticed you each doing these things well. Scott, (tentatively) I also heard you saying that you felt Jill was negative? Is that right?"

Scott: Umm (looking at the list of speaker skills)…yes, like…I was offering suggestions to help with where the baby will sleep but she didn't think any of the options were any good."

Educator: So Scott, you seem to be saying that you would have liked Jill to use more of the skill: describe positives, is that right?

Scott: Yes, I think so. She just seems to dismiss whatever I suggest, and I feel like I cannot say anything useful.

Jill: I guess I could do more positives – sometime I feel so overwhelmed and tired…

Educator: I noticed Scott that you seemed to notice Jill was feeling overwhelmed and you were offering solutions to the problem. Perhaps Jill is after something other than just a solution.

Scott: [Nods.] Like what?

Educator: I wonder if you, Scott, could think of another listener skill you could have used instead of offering solutions?

Scott: Ahh-hah…(nodding)… maybe this is a time I should be asking about feelings, and maybe the listener skill paraphrasing feelings?

Practice Tip

The goal of dialog with the couple about communication is to help each partner list skills accurately, identify strengths, stay in their speaker/listener role for a bit to test out skills; and explore skills each partner could do more of to help the conversation.

Giving and Receiving Feedback

This unit in Couple CARE for Parents also addresses giving and receiving feedback. Feedback is defined as discussing with your partner your ideas about their strengths and also your suggestions for change in their behavior. Giving and receiving feedback is also a useful skill for couples to do well. Partners often have useful suggestions on their partners' strengths, and areas for them to work on in their communication. However, it is important that feedback is given in a constructive, positive way that is easy for the partner to hear. Table 3.4 provides some guidelines for giving and receiving feedback and can be reviewed with couples to help them learn the tips for giving and receiving feedback.

The communication self-evaluation activity provides a sample of communication, which couples can use to reflect on their partner's communication strengths and areas to work on. We suggest following the skills self-rating with an exercise in giving and receiving feedback. Ask individuals to write down two positives about how their partner communicated and one suggestion for change. Then ask the couple to give each other feedback. Some useful pointers to give couples about feedback are as follows. (1) Most people appreciate positive feedback about what they do well. (2) Criticism tends to make a partner feel defensive, and they are more likely to disagree with the feedback or justify it. Further, they are less likely to listen to criticism. (3) Most people are likely to listen to suggestions (but less likely to listen to a demand) for change if it is shared sensitively and kindly.

Table 3.4 Guidelines for giving and receiving feedback

Giving feedback works best when:	Receiving feedback works best when:
1. The feedback starts with positive comments about your partner's communication strengths 2. Suggestions for change are offered rather than criticisms 3. Suggestions for change are offered gently, as ideas to consider 4. You ask for reactions to the feedback (e.g., What do you think of that suggestion?)	1. You listen to all the feedback and do not interrupt 2. You use your listener skills to really understand the feedback 3. You avoid becoming defensive 4. You consider the feedback. Think about whether there is some truth in it and if you agree or disagree 5. You suggest a plan for how you will respond to the feedback

Clinical Connection
Can you think of a time when you received helpful feedback? What was it about helpful feedback that made it easy to hear? What about a time when you received unhelpful feedback—can you identify what made it unhelpful?

Table 3.5 Less helpful and more helpful feedback examples

Less helpful feedback	Reason why it is less helpful	More helpful feedback
"I really like the way we talked together just then"	Very vague. Giving specific behavioral examples would be better	"I really liked how you paid attention to what I was saying, you looked interested and asked me questions. It made me feel you cared"
"You have to use summarizing content and feelings"	This is an instruction. People tend to respond better to suggestions than instructions	"I think I would like it if you used some of the listener skill summarizing content and summarizing feeling. Do you think you could try that and I can see if it makes me feel more heard?"
"You are always talking over me"	This is a criticism. Changing it into a suggestion for change, spoken in a kind voice, is much likely to be received well	"I find it hard to talk with you when you are interrupting me and I eventually stop trying to talk. Would it be okay if we tried to find a way for us to be better at turn-taking—like me giving you a signal that I have finished talking before you say your next thought?"

Table 3.5 contains examples of more helpful and less helpful feedback. This can be useful to assist couples who are struggling to be specific and positive in their feedback to each other. If running this session with a group of couples, educators could ask couples to brainstorm similar examples that can be written up on a whiteboard. Alternatively, an educator could share some examples of helpful and less helpful feedback and ask the partners to comment on whether they think it is a helpful or less helpful example of feedback, and what makes it helpful or less helpful.

Let us return to the transcript of the educator working with Jill and Scott. In the following section, the couples are assisted to discuss how they gave each other feedback about their communication skills.

Educator: "Now that we have done the self-evaluation of your communication skills let's look at the skill of giving and receiving feedback well. You've already started sharing some ideas of how your partner could change their communication. For example, Scott, I remember you saying that Jill seemed dismissive of some ideas and negative in the previous conversation. When you look at your communication skills handout what feedback could you give to Jill?

Scott: I see that I am supposed to come up with two positives and one suggestion for change.

Educator: Yep, that's right. Do you have some feedback you would like to give Jill about her communication skills?

Scott: Yeah…So I agree she is good at describing specifics and self-disclosing feelings, and a suggestion for change would be to include more of the skill describing positive.

Educator: Great, and what about you Jill. What feedback would you give Scott about his communication skills in the conversation you just had?

Jill: I think you were really good at paying attention, with nodding, staying on the topic, and even though it is not listed here you were good at suggesting solutions and it helped a bit, but I think I might like more reassurance, support about how I am feeling, a hug… that sort of thing.

Educator: I am wondering if the suggestion for change you are making Jill is asking for some paraphrasing feelings? Something like "You have been feeling so tired, overwhelmed by preparing for the baby's arrival and how nothing seems to be the right thing to do."

Jill: Yeah. [Nodding].

Educator: You are both getting the hang of this. Just before I leave to check in on another couple do you have any questions? (Jill and Scott shake their heads), OK, to finish off the exercise I wonder if you could have a try at giving each other this feedback about each other's communication skills, see how it goes to be the receiver of the feedback.

Practice Tip
Some people find listening quite challenging, they persistently interrupt, disagree or change the focus of the discussion. In such instances the speaker–listener floor exercise can be helpful. In this procedure one partner is given the "floor". (It can be helpful to have a piece of paper (or carpet) to symbolize the floor.) The speaker is asked to make brief statements, and to pause to let the listener paraphrase. The listener has to paraphrase what the speaker says, and not to interrupt, disagree or rebut. The speaker hangs onto the floor until she or he feels understood, and then passes the floor to their partner.

Communication Self-Change

Couple CARE for Parents (CCP) includes education that introduces ideas and skills to help couples have a satisfying relationship, and jointly to manage the challenges of parenthood. CCP also has experiential exercises that prompt reflection by the partners on the application of these ideas and skills to the couple's own relationship. Another key component of CCP is to have each partner engage in self-change, which means each person selecting one thing they want to work on to enhance their relationship based on the ideas introduced in particular units. Self-change is encouraged through having people develop a self-change plan, and later reviewing the success of implementing that self-change plan.

Self-change plans are a central element of Couple CARE for Parents and appear at the end of each unit. At the start of the following unit the implementation of the self-change plan is reviewed. The primary intent of the self-change plan is to facilitate couples applying what they learn through CCP to their relationship. Participants choose what aspect(s) of the content covered they find most relevant, and apply that idea or skill in their relationship. This self-directed learning approach is based on research that adult learners almost always select what they see as relevant from any learning and selectively focus on and apply that content (Lizzio & Wilson, 2004). In CCP we accept that is what people do, and make the process of selection of goals explicit. Having the learners state explicitly what they see as important has the advantage of allowing the educator to understand participants' thoughts on the content. It helps them to formulate self-change goals that are meaningful to them, and that are likely to be effective in enhancing the couple relationship.

The focus is on self-change, of changing one's own behavior, as a means to improving the couple's relationship. There are three reasons for this focus. First, it is more in one's personal control to change one's own behavior than to bring about change in another person's behavior. Second, people usually are inspired to make effort to enhance their relationship when they see their partner making an effort. Thus self-change often sets off a virtuous cycle of each partner seeking to do their bit for the relationship (Halford, 2011). Finally, we know that distressed couples often attribute relationship difficulties to their partner (Halford, 2001). Learning to take appropriate responsibility for one's behavior within the relationship and actively using self-change to enhance the relationship is an important skill. Couples who have high levels of these self-change skills, which we call relationship self-regulation, are likely to sustain high relationship satisfaction across time (Halford et al., 2007).

The self-change plans are based on Halford's (2001) relationship self-regulation concept. Self-regulation refers to those processes that enable an individual to guide his/her goal-directed activities over time and across changing circumstances (contexts). Regulation implies modulation of thought, affect, behavior, or attention via deliberate or automated use of specific mechanisms and supportive meta-skills. Relationship self-regulation means that partners attend to the relationship, the factors that influence their relationship, and engage in effective action to promote relationship satisfaction.

Table 3.6 is a blank self-change plan that sets out the four-step structure used to promote relationship self-regulation. The steps are as follows: (1) DESCRIBE the issue in clear and specific terms that the person wants to work on. (2) FOCUS on that person's own current behavior, evaluating the pluses and minuses of what they currently do. (3) SET GOAL is to define a clear specific action that will be done. (4) EVALUATE is reviewing how the self-change plan went.

More specifically, in the DESCRIBE section partners are asked to think about how their relationship is going, to choose one thing they would like to improve, and then write clearly what it is they want to work on. Educators should help partners focus their self-change plans on key areas that really make a difference to relationships (so far we have covered parenting expectations, mutual support, and couple communication).

Table 3.6 Self-change plan

On your own pick one area in your relationship that you would like to improve that involves changing something about your behavior. Choose an area that is important to you. Follow the four steps below. If this exercise seems difficult at first, do not worry, as your educator will review the self-change steps with you

1. **DESCRIBE** Describe the issue you would like to work on clearly and positively	2. **FOCUS** Describe what you currently do .... What are the **pluses** of your current behavior? .... What are the **minuses** of your current behavior? ....
3. **SET GOAL** Define exactly what I want to do. Where and when will I do it? .... What might get in the way? How will I make sure it happens?	4. **EVALUATE—Afterward:** What did I actually do? .... What positives resulted? .... What negatives resulted? .... What do I do from here? ....

In the second step of self-change partners are asked to FOCUS on their own behavior. Partners are asked to think about what they currently do (not what their partner does). The person writes down the pluses and minuses of how they currently behave. This process achieves several things. First, people tend to behave in particular ways for understandable reasons. For example, someone not talking about a particular issue with their partner might be because they are concerned that a discussion might provoke conflict. By recognizing the pluses of current behavior (not talking avoids conflict) we acknowledge the reasons for behaving in the current manner. Then the minuses of that behavior can be identified (e.g., the issue does not get resolved). Balancing up the pluses and minuses can build motivation to change (e.g., we really do need to talk about this issue), and suggest potential goals (e.g., to raise the topic in such a way as to make conflict unlikely).

Asking people to focus on their own behavior does not mean they ignore what their partner does. But, it does mean that behavior change starts with what **each individual can do**. If a person is really focused on getting their partner to change something, then often it can be useful to have the person reflect on the behavior they have used till now to try to influence their partner to change. Since they are still seeking change from their partner the current influencing behavior is ineffective, and so the goal might be to try different ways of seeking to influence the partner. Three things that often people have often not tried when seeking to promote change in their spouse are as follows. First, ask the partner about their views on whatever the desired change is and really listen. Perhaps there is a compelling reason the partner has not changed. Second, ask if there is anything they can do to support or assist the partner to make the change. For example, one woman was upset that her husband agreed to do more of the cooking but just did not carry through. When she asked if she could support him in doing more cooking he asked for help as he felt self-conscious about his lack of cooking skills. They agreed to share some cooking together to develop his skills. (He was so inspired he then enrolled in a couple of cooking classes and learned some recipes he then taught to his wife.) Third, make a change yourself that your spouse has asked for. Sometimes showing you are working to address your partner's wishes motivates them to make your needs a higher priority for them. (The husband who cooked more was surprised by his wife a few weeks later when she booked them into a cabin in the mountains for a romantic weekend.)[1]

The third step of self-change is SET GOAL. It is important that the educator help participants shape up their self-change plans to be specific actions that the person can reasonably achieve in the next week or two. For example, if one partner's goal is "to be more loving," ask what specific things he/she can do in the next week that will express loving.

Table 3.7 has a set of guidelines on how to develop effective self-change plans with examples of poorly and well-worded self-change plans. It can be very useful to

Table 3.7 How to write a self-change plan

Definition	Poor example	Good example
Clear: being specific and concrete about what happens and when	We sometimes fight We never have time to see each other	After work on busy days, I tend to argue about little things such as whose turn it is to cook On weekends we each have lots of things we do. We have not gone out as a couple, just the two of us, for 7 weeks. I want to go out together more than that
Positive: think about what you do want, not what you don't want in the relationship. Avoid blaming the other person for things you do not like	I hate the way we never spend any time together	I would like to spend more time with my partner
Specific: be precise rather than vague about your action plan. Try to focus on behaviors that can be seen	I want to feel closer my partner	I would like discuss my work and hobbies, which are important to me, with my partner
Realistic: select actions you are likely to be able to do	I will never get angry again I will shower my partner with presents	I will try to be calm, to listen to her and speak quietly, when we next talk about this issue Tomorrow I will stop at the shops on the way home from work and buy my partner something I know she'll like—a mango
Time-limited: define when you will do your actions	From now on I will cuddle my partner more	This week, I will cuddle my partner for a few minutes each morning before I get out of bed

[1] There is a finding in the research that when men contribute equitably to household chores and child care, the couple tend to have a more active and mutually satisfying sexual relationship. This can be a useful point to make to men and women.

Table 3.8 Example of a completed self-change plan

1. **DESCRIBE** *I would like to spend more quality time with my wife. We are always so busy, and I forget to prioritize spending time with her*	2. **FOCUS** *I am working, keeping up with the housework and yard work, seeing family and friends. I play footie and go to the gym* Pluses: *I am pretty happy I can manage to do all of the above* Minuses: *I am feeling distant from my wife*
3. **SET GOAL** *Tonight I will ask my wife to come on a dinner out this Friday night, followed by an evening stroll along the river. I will ask her about how she is and really listen to her answer* *If she is busy or too tired I will check if she wants to do lunch on Sunday instead, or next Friday. Or ask her what and when she would like to spend quality time with me*	3. **EVALUATE** *I asked her out* Positive: *She said yes. We had a really nice dinner and the weather was perfect for a walk along the river* Negative: *It felt a bit awkward at first asking her questions and really listening—like I was trying too hard (but then we relaxed and it was nice)*

refer to this handout and work through it with the couple before asking them to formulate a self-change plan. As this is the first self-change plan the couple have been asked to develop, working with the partners enables the educator to assess their understanding of the self-change plan idea, and to refine their skills in self-change.

Once steps 1–3 are written, the partner needs to implement the self-change plan, ideally within the next week, and then complete step 4. EVALUATE requires the partner to reflect on the success of the self-change plan and includes answering questions such as: Did you do what you said you would do? What effect did it have on your relationship? We describe the process of reviewing self-change plans in detail in Chap. 4.

An example of a completed self-change plan is presented in Table 3.8. If participants are struggling to finalize a self-change plan it can be useful to show them this handout as an example.

Managing Common Challenges in Running this Unit

One Partner is a Substantially Better Communicator than the Other

Such an imbalance can make the less skilled communicator feel uncomfortable or incompetent, and the more skilled communicator frustrated. In such instances it is often helpful to tell the couple that some people find learning intimate communication to be more challenging than others, and that is perfectly understandable. The most important thing is to work at improving communication as best one can.

The fact that one is trying seems to do as much good for a relationship as achieving any particular standard. It also is worth noting that in most couples the partners bring different strengths to a relationship. One partner might be more effective at expressing feelings, the other partner better at remaining calm in a crisis, or having certain useful practical skills—like earning or managing money, or doing home maintenance. An important advantage of being in a couple relationship is that partners can, to some extent, specialize in what they do best. In truly great relationships each partner recognizes the strengths of their spouse, and accepts their human fallibilities.

Mistaking Hearing for Listening

Some participants can be looking away, not responding to what their partner is saying, perhaps even attending to something else, and yet state, "I am listening, I can hear them." Hearing is the physical process of recognizing sound. Listening is an active process of looking at the other person, thinking about what the person is saying, really trying to understand, and communicating that attempt to listen in an active way. If someone is unsure about what is meant by active listening it can be useful to show them. Ask the person to talk about something they are interested in and the educator should start by not listening (e.g., look away, glace at your watch, give no active encouragement as the listener), and after a minute or so state you are going to change and then use very active listening. Ask the person to describe the change in the educator's behavior (get them to be specific about particular behaviors like where the educator was looking, what they said, etc.). Then ask them about the experience of being heard versus being really listened to by someone else. Participants can then try using active listening with their own spouse.

One Partner is a Wordy Speaker

Some people describe things in a long, detailed manner, bringing a lot of tangential material to their statements. This can make it very difficult for the listener to extract the key message. Some people tell a story as they experienced it, rather than extracting the key points they really wanted to communicate. Shaping people up to be brief, and to emphasize the core intended message is important. Consider the following example of Melanie and Roland's discussion that was supposed to be on expectations about becoming parents.

Melanie: I was at the doctors last week for my regular check-up, and I bumped into Rachel. You remember Rachel? She used to be a regular at the gym till she got pregnant, tall woman with dark hair?

Roland: Yeah, I remember. What about her?

Melanie: She is married to Jason, the IT fellow. I think it was IT anyway.
Roland: Jason? Don't remember him.
Melanie: He hardly came to the gym; he had to travel for work. Not sure why you would sign up for a fancy gym if you never use it. Anyway, where was I?
Roland: You saw Rachel?
Melanie: Yes, at the doctor's. She looked awful, I mean awful. She had big bags under her eyes. She has put on weight, a lot of weight. And you remember how proud she was of her fitness? Well she came up a short flight of stairs and she was puffing and blowing. Well I asked how being a parent was going, her little Aisha is six months old, can you believe it? Well she just burst into tears, the poor woman. She used to be such a strong character and well ..."
Roland: Where is this story going Mel?
Educator: Roland, you seem a little lost.
Roland: I am, I have no idea what this story is about.
Educator: Melanie, your story has lots of detail and it seems Roland is having trouble following your point. Can you say one key thing you are trying to get across?
Melanie: It frightened me, seeing this once strong woman falling apart.
Educator: Are you saying you are worried this might happen to you after your baby is born?
Melanie: I just don't know how I will cope. I don't know anything about babies.
Educator: So you are a bit scared about how you will manage as a mother. Understandable, very understandable, becoming parent is a big change. Can you tell Roland how seeing Rachel affected you, and try to say it in two to three sentences so it makes it easy for Roland to understand your key point.

In the example, the educator helps the speaker to clarify their message, and then prompts the speaker to be brief. Sometimes it takes multiple rounds of summarizing and shaping to help people become clearer speakers. Importantly by the educator listening and helping the speaker refine her message the speaker reveals an important feeling, which now the husband has a chance to understand.

A Participant Reports that Trying to Communicate Differently Does Not Feel "Natural"

Feeling slightly uncomfortable often occurs when people are pushing themselves to try something different. Feeling natural happens when something has been practiced so much that it requires little conscious effort; it has become a habit. Most people feel "natural" when they drive a car because they have practiced driving so often they do not have to consciously process the steps. However, as anyone who has ever learned to drive a car, or learned another language as an adult, or learned to play a musical instrument, will attest these skills do not feel natural at the start. Any competent guitarist has spent thousands of hours learning the basics so they can play music without having to consciously think where a particular chord or note is on the instrument. In the same way, with practice people learn the communication habits required to feel natural. Importantly, as people develop good communication habits, they then find their own voice to use the skill in their own way, just as great guitarists add their own distinctive style.

A Participant Struggles to Identify a Self-Change Issue

Couples may need the educator's assistance in identifying an issue to address. For couples who are highly satisfied there might be little they feel the need to change. It is entirely legitimate for couples to identify the strengths they see in their relationship, and the focus might be on sustaining strengths. The educator can focus the discussion on how to sustain positives in the relationship, with a focus on managing this as the couple become parents. For example, if a couple identifies they have a lot of fun together it would be useful to review the ways they have had fun till now and how having a child might require adaptation to sustain the fun. For some participants self-change will focus on behaviors they already do that make a positive contribution to their relationship and which they could do more often. Examples of such small positives include buying flowers or chocolate for their partner, rubbing their partner's back, expressing appreciation to their partner, sitting with their partner talking about their day and actively listening, or offering to cook dinner.

Chapter 4
Conflict Management

Chapter Highlights

This chapter describes how to do the following:

- Introduce the importance of managing differences effectively.
- Review with couples their current patterns of conflict management.
- Introduce the idea of conflict management ground rules, and have couples identify ground rules that will be useful in their relationship.
- Have each partner self-evaluate their conflict communication skills.
- Explore how each partner currently recovers after a conflict.
- Help each partner develop a conflict self-change plan.

This unit of Couple CARE for Parents is focused on managing differences. The unit begins with a review of the implementation of the communication self-change plan from the previous unit. Then there is an introduction of the importance of managing differences effectively, both to help use partner differences as relationship assets and to avoid destructive conflict. The couple is asked to identify topic areas that currently are a source of disagreement between them, and current patterns of interaction the partners use when discussing these areas of difference. The concept of conflict ground rules is introduced, and couples are asked to identify some ground rules they want to use in their relationship to manage conflict effectively. Then the couple discusses a difficult topic and self-evaluates their communication when discussing a topic that is a source of disagreement. The penultimate exercise addresses helping the relationship recover after conflict. Finally, each partner formulates a self-change plan to enhance their conflict management.

Electronic Supplementary Material: The online version of this chapter (doi:10.1007/978-1-4939-1613-9_4) contains supplementary material, which is available to authorized users.

W.K. Halford et al., *Clinical Guide to Helping New Parents*,
Springer Series on Couples and Health, DOI 10.1007/978-1-4939-1613-9_4

Couples rate learning communication and conflict management as the most valuable aspects of skill-based relationship education (Stanley 2001; Wilson & Halford, 2008). Helping couples manage conflict better is one of the more challenging aspects of the program for educator(s) to deliver. Couples need to be able to discuss their differences without experiencing destructive conflict, and the educator needs to create the context that allows couples to do that. The educator needs to be ready to intervene quickly if a couple is experiencing escalating negativity, and to guide them back to more constructive methods of communication, which is relatively easy in a one-on-one home visit or clinic appointment. In a group context this requires that there are sufficient numbers of educators for the number of couples (we suggest at least one educator for each four couples), so that the educators can closely monitor how each couple is progressing. If the couple is completing this unit at home with a telephone follow-up call from the educator it can be helpful to ask the couple to restart the conversation for 2–3 min while the educator listens. This provides a sample of the couple's communication that the couple and educator can use to discuss the conflict management pattern, and partners' communication skills. That allows the educator to explore the accuracy of each partner's conflict management skills self-evaluation, and to shape those self-evaluations as required.

Practical Issues in Home-Based Delivery of the Program

If Couple CARE for Parents is delivered as we recommend, then the current unit will be delivered in a home visit. This means the couple completes exercises at home with the educator present. We recommend the home visit where feasible as this helps the couple to develop the habit of working on the program at home. In the current unit and the one that follows immediately after the birth the educator is present to assist the couple with the exercises. In the final three units the program is completed in flexible delivery mode, where the couple completes the exercises on their own, and the educator reviews their work by telephone or Internet video-conference. Table 4.1 sets out the tasks couples are asked to do that form part of this unit. The educator should have handouts for the couple in order to complete the tasks.

It is important to establish some ground rules around the home visit to ensure it is conducted effectively. The educator should discuss these ground rules with the couple by telephone before the sessions commence. First, the session is a formal appointment with a professional and should start and finish on time. It will take about 80 min. Both partners must be at home and available for the whole appointment. The session works best in a quiet, private space such as the kitchen table or living room. Televisions, computers, and mobile devices should be switched off. Second, if there is a dog in the house it must be secured away before the educator arrives. Third, the educator will telephone the couple prior to arrival to ensure both partners are at home, and call their supervisor/colleague to advise they are about to start the session. Fourth, the educator will call the supervisor/colleague when the session is complete, and they have gotten into their car to leave the home. Finally, the couple needs to set aside time for the review session, so both partners can participate without distraction.

Table 4.1 Content and activities for conflict management unit
Couple CARE for Parents is designed to be convenient for busy couples to do. So some of the content we give to you to complete at home in your own time. Your educator will review how you went in the appointment made with you. For this unit you are asked to do the following:

Topic and aim	Task	Handout
Promote self-change	Complete communication self-change plan	Communication Self-Change Plan
Identify current patterns of conflict management	Mark down and discuss the conflict management pattern you and your partner currently use	Patterns of Conflict Management
Conflict management ground rules	Discuss and select conflict management ground rules you wish to employ	Ground Rules for Conflict Management
Self-evaluate conflict management skills	Discuss an issue you disagree about with your partner and self-evaluate your conflict management communication	Conflict Communication Skills Self-Assessment
Recover from conflict	Review the recovery from conflict self-talk example	Example negative and positive self-talk
Develop conflict management self-change	Write down a conflict management self-change plan	Self-change plan

The guidelines we suggest are important for safety. Often our educators travel alone to couples' homes at night. (Some agencies might prefer to send two educators as an extra safety precaution, but that is expensive.) The guidelines also are important to ensure that the sessions are effective.

Reviewing Communication Self-Change

The review of the communication self-change plan is the first time the educator has the chance to assist partners with implementing changes they have selected. It is important to prompt each partner to reflect on what they have done, and its relationship impact. Some useful questions to pose of partners, which can be used with couples in a home visit or a telephone call, are as follows: "*What stands out in your mind as the most important part of what we have covered in Couple CARE for Parents so far? How might you apply ideas from our exploration of communication to your relationship? How did you do with last week's self-change plan? Can you tell me exactly what you tried to do? On a scale from 0 to 10 (with 0 being "did not do anything like I planned" to 10 "completed exactly what I intended") how well would you rate your carrying through of your self-change plan?*" If the person did as they planned, then the following questions are useful: "*What benefit, if any, was there for your relationship or your partner from you doing this? What else do you plan to do to follow up on this?*"

As an illustration of this review process, consider the following brief transcript in which Kathleen is describing her attempts to show greater appreciation for her partner Morrie's contribution around the house.

Educator: "Kathleen, what exactly did you set out to do?"
Kathleen: "I wanted to recognize more what Morrie does around the place."

Educator: "Hmm, hmm, great. And how did that go? *Can you tell me exactly what you tried to do?*"

Kathleen: "Great. Morrie cooked on Thursday might, which is when I work late. Not only that but he cleaned up as well, and I made a special point of thanking him."

Educator: "You expressed thanks, terrific. And what sort of response did you get from Morrie?"

Kathleen: "Well, even though Morrie knew thanking him was my plan, he still seemed really pleased."

Educator: "We can all do with a genuine 'thank you'. Knowing that being thanked meant something to Morrie. So, on a scale from 0 to 10 (with 0 being "did not do anything like I planned" to 10 "completed exactly what I intended") how well would you rate your carrying through of your self-change plan?"

Kathleen: "I rate it as a 9 out of 10. I definitely did the plan."

Educator: "Great, what will you do to make sure you keep doing this?"

Kathleen: "Watch for Morrie being positive, and keep commenting on it at least a couple of times."

Educator: "Great plan. Let's check in a week or two, just to see how you're going with that idea."

Kathleen carried out her self-change plan, and felt some real benefit from it. A limitation of what she did was a lack of any specific strategy to maintain expression of appreciation. For some people just making the resolution is enough. Other people might need to practice expression of appreciation a number of times for that behavior to become an ingrained habit. The educator signals they will check back to see how Kathleen is doing in carrying through on her resolution. It is important to keep reviewing people's self-change attempts, and helping them develop sustained effort to strengthen their relationship with their partner.

For people who successfully completed their self-change plan it is helpful to explore the success. Questions like the following can be used: "*What was the difficult part, if anything, in carrying out your communication self-change plan? What effect did changing your communication have on the conversation with your partner? What have you learned from this in terms of what you want to do in the future?*" It can also be helpful to ask the spouse to comment on any positive benefit she or he sees from the self-change. If the effect of self-change was positive, the educator can build on this success, asking the person how they might sustain further positive impacts of such change on the relationship. In responding to the completion of self-change plans it is important to praise and support people's change efforts. Even partial attempts should be given encouragement; as they reflect effort to enhance the relationship.

If the current unit is run as a group session it can be helpful to have people write down answers to these questions, and the educator can circulate among the couples, discussing their answers with them. Having couples report back to the group on what they tried to change and their successes is also useful to do. Whatever the specific process of reviewing self-change plans, it is important to emphasize that participants should seek to be constructive, to praise each other's self-change efforts, and to offer any suggestions tentatively.

Sometimes self-change plans are implemented, but do not have the effects that were intended. It is important to help people see the process of self-change as one of experimentation, of exploring what is most helpful in enhancing their relationship. If this spirit of experimentation is encouraged, then people keep learning important things when they make an effort, regardless of the immediate effect on the relationship. For example, in the following brief transcript, the educator is reviewing Pablo's attempt to organize a date with Gemma, which had not worked out as Pablo had hoped.

Educator: "What was your plan Pablo?"

Pablo: "To organize a special night. Gemma has been really tired in the last month or so, so I planned to cook a nice meal for us at home. Just relax with good food. I cooked Spanish paella, just to try something different. But Gemma felt a bit nauseous, and I made a really rich sauce with seafood and she did not eat much and then felt unwell. My meal was a fizzer."

Educator: "Fizzer?"

Pablo: "Yeah, it was too rich, she didn't enjoy any of the food, and had quite an upset tummy at the end of the night. Not really the relaxing dinner that I had in mind."

Educator: "You put in a lot of effort by the sound of it, trying to cook a new recipe. When you try new things, sometimes it doesn't work out as you'd hoped. What have you learned from this?"

Pablo: "Well, Gemma is off food a bit at the moment, the doc says women in the last few months of pregnancy often do not feel like eating much."

Educator: "I remember you saying earlier how important food is to you, and that you might have got in a rut with the foods you eat. So seeking out new things to cook seems good, but it did not work out quite as you wanted this time. So what happens next?"

Pablo: "Small serves of simple Italian?" (laughs).

Educator: "Sure, why not? Is that seriously what you want to try?"

Pablo: "Yeah, I think so."

Discussing Incomplete Self-Change Efforts

When self-change plans have not been implemented it is important to problem solve, and assist people to set themselves up for future success. The educator undertaking the review process provides a model of how to conduct self-change, as well as assisting the couple to produce positive shifts in the relationship. Each partner learning self-change is central to sustaining long-term couple relationship satisfaction.

It is well established that successful completion of homework assignments is associated with substantially more benefits from psychological programs (Kazantzis,

Table 4.2 Some questions to explore non-completion of self-change plans

Area being explored	Possible questions
Does the person have the knowledge and skills to undertake the task?	*Just to make sure we were clear, tell me what you intended to do in your self-change plan.* (Probe as required to establish exactly what was to be done and when.) *If you were going to do that, show me how you would start.* (For example, have the person ask a question that starts a conversation.)
Do the person's cognitions promote task completion?	*Sometimes people have second thoughts about their self-change plan. What really is your thinking about doing the task?* Probe as to whether the person believes the task is useful, is likely to make a difference to the relationship
Does the environment promote task completion?	*Was there anything unusual about the past week that made it hard to get the task done? Is there anything extra you can set in place that would make it easier for you to do this?* Probe for exactly where and when the task might be attempted

Deane, Ronan, & L'Abate, 2005). Therefore, it is very important to carefully review lack of action on a self-change plan with participants. It is easy for individuals to feel criticized when reviewing non-completion of tasks, and this can lead to defensiveness, which is not productive. Hence, the review needs to be positively focused and refine the self-change plan to make it workable.

A useful approach to exploring non-completion of self-change plans is described in Table 4.2. This approach is based on Kazantzis et al.'s (2005) suggestions on common sources of failing to complete behavioral assignments. Essentially, they suggest that there are three common reasons why people fail to do tasks that they state they want to complete. First, individuals may be unclear about exactly what they are to do, or lack the skills to carry out the task. A common example of a lack of skill interfering with successful completion of a task is if a partner resolves to be a better listener to their spouse, but lacks the communication skills to convey effective listening. The questions suggested in Table 4.2 enable the educator to identify if either lack of understanding or lack of skill is the reason for an unsuccessful attempt at self-change. The second possibility is that particular thoughts about completing the task interfere with performance. For example, the person might believe that the self-change goal was not really useful. It is important to probe the person about what they really think about the self-change task. If the person has the requisite knowledge and skills, and believes the task is useful, then the third reason for unsuccessful self-change is possible. It is likely something in the person's environment that is the problem. There might not be a specific environmental, or situational prompt that gets the person started. This is often what people mean when they say they "forgot" or "did not get around to it."

The following transcript illustrates the process of how an educator can review non-completion of a self-change plan. In this case Janine has just reported that she did not "get around to" arranging a planned weekend trip to buy things for the nursery.

Educator: "Janine, what were you trying to do?"

Janine: "It was a busy week, and it just did not happen."

Educator: "Okay Janine so it didn't happen. Just to be sure that I was clear when we were talking, can you tell you exactly what it was that you intended to do across the week?"

Janine: "I was going to find a couple of places for us to go to on the weekend to look for a cot, and a change table."

Educator: "Okay, and what exactly were you wanting to get done by tonight so you two could do this?"

Janine: "I was going to call a couple of places to see what they stock. We went to a place a couple of weeks ago and all they had was baby clothing, no crib or anything."

Educator: "Okay that seems pretty clear. Now sometimes when people get to the point of actually taking some action they start to wonder if it's really a good idea. What do you <u>really</u> think about the idea of organizing a baby gear buying trip for the weekend?"

Janine: "I liked the idea. We've had very little time to plan for the baby's arrival and its getting close now. But I worry if we have got enough money to be buying all this stuff. Our house repayments are pretty high. We're kind of struggling to keep up and maybe a whole lot of gear is just beyond us now."

Educator: "Mmm hmm, Mmm hmm. So it might just be a bit much money? So what do you want to do?"

Janine: "I think Geoff and I should sit down and review our budget. See what sort of stuff we really can afford."

Educator: "Excellent, excellent. So you could do a review. If you can afford what you would really like, great. If not, maybe there's something else that you could find, which is not quite so expensive."

Janine: "Mmm hmm."

Educator: "So Janine what will you do in the next week?"

Janine: [Turning to Geoff] "How about we sit down one night this week, go through the budget, and see if we've got a few hundred that we can afford to spend on the weekend?"

Educator: "Geoff?"

Geoff: "I think we probably can afford the stuff we want, but let's check and see."

Educator: "Janine, it seems to me that just thinking about going shopping on the weekend away had moved things along. It's got you thinking about how you and Geoff can prepare for your baby's arrival in an affordable way."

In the above example, Janine had a thought that interfered with her self-change plan of organizing a shopping trip on the weekend. She had doubts that she and Geoff could really afford the cost. By identifying the blocking thought, the educator helped her to develop a way forward. In other instances the person might really want to carry out the self-change plan, and yet not get around to it. In busy lives, it can be easy for people to let relationship resolutions slip. If this were the case for Janine, it could be useful to discuss what she might do to make her self-change plan happen. For example, she and Geoff could identify a specific day, time, and place to have the planned conversation, or book in time in her diary (if she keeps one) to go shopping, or put a note on the fridge to remind them.

Practice Tip
In order for participants to be likely to complete homework assignments, it is crucial the participant is actively involved in developing the self-change plan they are to implement. Ask each person what they want to do to address a particular issue, rather than telling the person what you think should be done.

In responding to the completion of self-change plans it is important to praise and support people's change efforts. Even partial attempts should be given encouragement; as they reflect effort to enhance the relationship. In the above example, the educator praises Janine for having thought about what she intended to do. When self-change plans have not been implemented it is important to problem solve, and assist people to set themselves up for future success. The educator undertaking the review process provides a model of how to conduct self-change, as well as assisting the couple to produce positive shifts in the relationship. Each partner learning self-change is central to sustaining long-term couple relationship satisfaction.

The three-step review process described above is also helpful if the couple has "not got around" to completing any of the unit exercises when the program is delivered in flexible delivery mode. The educator can start by asking the couple what they understood they were going to do. Then the partners can be asked their real thoughts about doing those tasks. Lastly, the educator can explore how the couple could structure their time to get the tasks done. An important option open to educators is to work through the exercises with the couple, either in the home visit or via telephone or video-conference. While this approach takes more of the educator's time, it can be appropriate if couples are struggling to manage the materials.

Patterns of Conflict Management

Introducing the Importance of Managing Differences

The educator needs to introduce the value of differences between partners, and the importance of managing conflict effectively. You might do this with words like the following. "*People in good relationships tend to be healthier and happier than folks not in a relationship. One benefit of a good relationship is that you draw on the wisdom of two people, and the skills of two people, to manage life challenges. For example, suppose one partner tends to make decisions quickly, while the other partner is more reflective. When making large decisions, like buying a home or car, the two of them balance each other. The slower decision-making partner ensures that sufficient time is taken to consider the options, while the more decisive partner ensures they do not agonize for too long and miss opportunities. Perhaps one partner is a great cook but terrible with money, while the other is great with money but not such a good cook. The couple has both cooking and financial skills available to them. So differences between partners can be really useful.*"

It is useful to ask the couple to discuss some differences between the two of them that enhance their relationship. Examples of the sort of answers often generated include partners having complementary interests that enhance getting required tasks done (e.g., one person likes to cook, the other likes gardening); complementary role preferences (e.g., one partner is keen to pursue their career and enhance family income while the other prefers a home and family focus); and complementary skills (e.g., one person is good with budgeting and the other with decorating and making their home attractive).

A key point of this initial focus is to highlight that there are always differences between partners, and this has advantages. At the same time, differences can be a challenge to manage. Destructive conflict can arise if differences are not managed well, and the focus of Unit 4 is to help couples review and then enhance their management of differences.

Practice Tip
The research shows that conflict always occurs in couple relationships, and it is how the couples manage conflict that is crucial. It is often useful to make this point to couples.

Assessing Current Patterns of Managing Differences

Table 4.3 lists some common areas of disagreement between partners. Ask each partner to rate how often they disagree about these topics, and then discuss the ratings together. This helps couples identify the areas of disagreement that might need resolution. This identification of difficult topics can be very helpful to guide you on what issues couples need particular help discussing. It also suggests topics you can ask the couple to discuss in the conflict management communication self-evaluation exercise later in this unit.

Table 4.4 describes four common patterns of conflict management, and asks the couple to rate how often they use these different patterns. When working with groups of couples, we usually introduce these different patterns before asking the partners to self-evaluate their own pattern(s). Here are some general observations to share with couples that help them make sense of these patterns.

"*The demand-withdraw pattern often leaves the demander really frustrated. Have you ever had the experience of really wanting to talk about something that is*

Table 4.3 Common areas of couple disagreement
Please indicate how often you and your partner agree or disagree about each topic below

	Always agree	Almost always agree	Disagree infrequently	Frequently disagree	Almost always disagree	Always disagree
1. Handling family finances	O	O	O	O	O	O
2. Matters of recreation	O	O	O	O	O	O
3. Religious matters	O	O	O	O	O	O
4. Demonstrations of affection	O	O	O	O	O	O
5. Friends	O	O	O	O	O	O
6. Sex relations	O	O	O	O	O	O
7. Conventionality (correct or proper behavior)	O	O	O	O	O	O
8. Philosophy of life	O	O	O	O	O	O
9. Ways of dealing with parents or in-laws	O	O	O	O	O	O
10. Aims, goals, and things believed important	O	O	O	O	O	O
11. Amount of time spent together	O	O	O	O	O	O
12. Making major decisions	O	O	O	O	O	O
13. Household tasks	O	O	O	O	O	O
14. Leisure time interests and activities	O	O	O	O	O	O
15. Career decisions	O	O	O	O	O	O
16. Other (please specify): ……………………..	O	O	O	O	O	O
17. Other (please specify): ……………… ………….	O	O	O	O	O	O

bugging you, but your partner just seems to be disengaged, not discussing this with you? There are lots of ways to withdraw. She or he might be watching television, reading the paper, trying to get out the door to do something, or changing the topic, and to just not listening – zoning out.

The withdrawer often experiences the discussion just like a rabbit in a spot light, dazzled, trapped, frozen and not able to escape. The more the demander talks and pushes to discuss an issue, the more pressured the withdrawer feels and the more the withdrawer pulls away. And what happens then? The demander pushes even harder. This is not a helpful approach to managing conflict.

Table 4.4 Patterns of conflict management
As a couple, rate which patterns apply to you as a couple when you talk about a problem (you might use more than one pattern)

Demand-Withdraw	Escalate
When a problem arises, one of us tries to talk (the demander). Often the demander will complain or criticize. The other person talks little, may not listen, leaves the room, or just refuses to discuss the issue (the withdrawer) Does this pattern apply to you two? ❑ Almost all of the time ❑ Most the time ❑ Sometimes ❑ Rarely ❑ Never The demander often feels frustrated and not listened to. The withdrawer often feels attacked and that talking achieves little. Demand-withdraw makes it difficult to understand each other or to solve problems	When we talk about a problem, we both blame, attack, and criticize each other. We tend not to listen to each other, and things can get heated Does this pattern apply to you two? ❑ Almost all of the time ❑ Most the time ❑ Sometimes ❑ Rarely ❑ Never When couples escalate nasty fights can result. Often problems are unsolved, and partners often have hurt feelings
Avoid	Validating
When a problem arises, we do not get around to talking, we avoid discussing the problem Does this pattern apply to you two? ❑ Almost all of the time ❑ Most the time ❑ Sometimes ❑ Rarely ❑ Never Avoidance often means conflict is not obvious, but partners can become irritated and distant from each other. The problems are rarely solved	We both talk about the problem, hear each other out, and suggest possible solutions Does this pattern apply to you two? ❑ Almost all of the time ❑ Most the time ❑ Sometimes ❑ Rarely ❑ Never In effective management both partner are active in the discussion. Both use effective listener and speaker skills. They usually feel that they can talk about and solve problems

The avoid pattern occurs when both partners avoid talking about difficult issues – they both are "withdrawn." It has one major advantage – at least in the short term – you avoid uncomfortable discussions. The problem is the issue never gets dealt with. Suppose money is a hot topic for a couple, as it is for many couples. Avoidance of talking about money typically means the couple does not develop an agreed upon budget, might not be clear on who is supposed to pay bills, or how the income coming into the house is divided up. Eventually the pile of unpaid bills, or the credit card going over the limit, or running out of money between pays, forces the couple to address the money problem. At this point the couple is under great pressure from the pile up of debts, and talking calmly to solve the problems often gives way to arguing. "How could you let your credit card get to the limit?" "Well how come you never pay the bills?" There are lots of issues that a couple just has to discuss, and avoidance just does not work in the long term.

Escalation is the most obvious of problems in managing conflict. You argue, maybe it is relatively mild, a little sarcasm is swapped for a criticism or two. Sometimes it might get more heated, which might involve some serious criticism, maybe a really nasty insult or some name calling in the heat of the moment. At worst, really nasty fights can occur, where partners trade insults and accusations; maybe it even escalates to physical aggression – pushing, slapping, shoving or even worse. Any sort of escalation tends to leave both partners feeling hurt and possibly angry. These types of fights can feed on themselves, like a fire getting out of control, and seriously damage a relationship.

These different negative patterns – of demand-withdraw, avoid, and escalate – can all occur in the one couple. Sometimes a bad fight involving escalation leads to avoidance of talking about a sensitive issue. Frustration at the demand-withdraw pattern can escalate to a nasty fight.

Effective conflict management is a skill; it can be learned just like any other skill. It involves both partners listening to each other, and being respectful of the other person's point of view. The aim in the current unit is to review how you currently manage conflict and to offer some suggestions about how you can use effective conflict management."

The activity has partners rate how often they use each of the four patterns of conflict management on the form in Table 4.4. The couple then discusses the strengths and the challenges in their current approaches to conflict management. The goal is to have them consider whether changing their pattern(s) of conflict management might be helpful. It also can be useful to mention that the couple will soon be asked to have a discussion about an area of disagreement, and identify what pattern of conflict management they use during that discussion.

Conflict Management Guidelines and Ground Rules

There are some useful guidelines and ground rules for managing conflict that couples often find helpful. Guidelines refer to suggestions of what couples can do while discussing conflict that make it easier to manage conflict effectively. Ground rules are a set of ideas that couples can agree upon before discussing areas of differences, which structure discussions and make it easier to maintain effective conflict management. This section of the unit introduces these ideas, and couples apply these ideas to their relationship in the sections that follow.

Conflict Management Guidelines

Table 4.5 sets out some conflict management skills, which can serve as a useful handout for couples. The first point reminds the couples to use the communication skills they were introduced to in the previous unit on communication. The idea of point 2 of Table 4.5 can be introduced with words like the following.

Table 4.5 Conflict management skills

1. Don't try to solve the problem too quickly
2. Use "I"-Statements (rather then "you" statements)
3. Use the Speaker-listener floor Technique
   - When speaking be brief, be clear, pause and let the listener respond
   - When listening, pay attention, summarize what you hear, do not express your own ideas (yet) or disagree
4. Use your communication skills
   - Hear your partner out
   - Provide specific/concrete descriptions of problem behavior
   - Attend to and encourage each other
   - Make specific positive requests for change

"A common mistake many couples make when managing a difference is to try to jump to a solution, they try to solve the problem too quickly. Suppose you are trying to pick where you will spend your next vacation, and that you and your partner have disagreed about holiday destinations in the past. Starting the conversation with 'I think we should go to X' is likely to lead to a dead end. In contrast, starting with 'what would you really like in our next holiday?' might help you to understand your partner's needs and then the two of you might come up with ideas that suit both of you.

In other words, it is really important that each partner listen effectively to the other, and ensure they truly understand the partner's perspective before trying to identify solutions. I often suggest to couples, if you really want to fix this problem, don't try to solve it. Instead focus on listening to your partner, find out how they see things. Seek first to understand, then to be understood."

A third important conflict management guideline is to ensure each partner gets to speak and to listen. A common mistake in couples who argue is that they both are speaking, and neither is listening effectively to the other. To overcome that habit, the speaker–listener technique can be useful. The essence of this technique is formalizing the speaker and listener roles, so both partners have a turn to speak. In face-to-face sessions it can be helpful to have a small piece of linoleum or carpet which acts as the "floor," and to demonstrate the idea. (If you are speaking by telephone or online video you can ask the couple to use a piece of paper as the floor.)

Table 4.5 includes guidelines for following the speaker and listener roles. It can be useful to remind people of the key points in this handout if you are using the speaker–listener procedure. An example of using the speaker–listener process is as follows with a couple discussing whether they need to change homes to prepare for their baby's arrival.

Educator: "Tasha, Mark this is the 'floor'. When you have the floor it is your chance to speak. As the speaker you need to explain your thinking about what you want in a place to live. If you don't have the floor, you're the listener. The listener only listens, meaning let the person finish what they have to say. Using the listener skills as described in the unit we did last month is useful. The listener is not to disagree or talk about their own ideas. The listener has to focus on what the person with the floor is saying, and summarize what the speaker is saying. Got that? OK, who is going to have the floor first? [Tasha extends her hand] OK, Tasha you have the floor. Mark, your job is to really listen to Tasha, maybe ask her some questions to make sure you get it. OK? Tasha, please tell Mark about your thoughts on where you want to live."

Tasha: "I really want us to have a nice place we can call home, you know with a garden, and a place for our child to run around, some space …"

Mark: "Uh-huh"

Tasha: "I just feel that our unit, you know stuck up in a high rise in the inner city, its not somewhere for a child to grow up."

Mark: "But a house in the suburbs is such high maintenance, we'll spend all our time gardening, painting, that's going to cut into our time with our child…"

Educator: "Mark, remember your job right now is to listen. In a few minutes you will get the floor, and then it's really important for you to explain some of the things you just started saying. But for now, what has Tasha just said to you?"

Mark: "That she wants to live in a house."

Educator: "Good, and why does she want to live in house?"

Mark: "Because of the space, the garden and stuff, for a kid to play in."

Educator: "Is there anything you want to ask her about what she has said?"

Mark: "Ah … [pause]"

Educator: [after a few seconds, offers…] "I am wondering what is important to her about this. How about asking her what she really likes about the idea of a house for a child."

Mark: "Tasha, what is about the house thing that so grabs you?"

Tasha: "It's the chance for us to build a place that really feels like ours. With all the moving around till now, I've never felt we put down roots, made somewhere our place. Now I want that, you know? Somewhere that our child can play, can have other kids come over and have a meal, which my mother can stay for weekends when we are under pressure. I want to grow herbs in the backyard, and have a seat under a tree, and be able to sit out and have a glass of wine in <u>our</u> place, watch our baby grow up."

Mark: "Hmmmm."

Educator: "Mark, can you summarize what Tasha just said."

Mark: "Well, she has this picture of our families visiting, of somewhere that sort of feels home like to her, of a place where our child can play and grow up."

Educator: "Great job, good summary. Tasha: do you think Mark has understood what you were saying?"

Tasha: "Yes. And it's really important to me, this building a home to raise our child in."

Mark: "Doesn't our unit feel like home?"

Tasha: "With the two of us there, yeah, but there's no room for a baby, or my Mum or your folks. And I want to garden, I like getting my hands into the soil and watching stuff grow. I want our child to be connected to the real world of plants, and sky"

Mark: "Yeah, you love wandering through the garden at your Mum's place – I know that. And its part of what you grew up with"

Educator: "Tasha, if you think Mark has got your key message, how about passing him the floor. [Tasha passes the floor to Mark]. OK, now Tasha it's your turn to listen. Go ahead Mark."

Mark: "I am worried that a house will take up all out time on weekends, you know gardening, looking after the place. And we won't have time to do things we really enjoy, and want to do as a family."

Tasha: "But we can plan a low maintenance garden, you know lots of native plants and stuff."

Educator: "Tasha, what did you just do?"

Tasha: "I started talking rather than listening?"

Educator: "Mmhmmm. So let's get back to what Mark said. Can you summarize."

Tasha: "Mark, you said that it might tie us up with chores on weekends."

Mark: "Yeah, I mean we both work hard during the week, and I want to be able to chill out, spend time with our baby, perhaps still get to see friends, do what we do now."

Tasha: "So you're worried that if we go into a house we become tied down with gardening and stuff and never get time for fun?"

Mark: "I am. I see lots of guys at work who seem to have nothing to talk about except child care, renovations and gardening. I don't want to get stuck in that suburban rut."

Tasha: "So you see a house as eating away at your interests, preventing you doing stuff you want to do?"

Educator: "Fantastic Tasha, good summary. It is interesting that as you two are talking we are hearing how important it is to Mark that he have time to maintain his range of interests, and Tasha is saying how much she values the idea of a home, which for her means a garden and space, room for a baby to play."

The aim in the above process was to have the couple understand the speaker and listener roles, and how to apply the floor technique to provide structure to a discussion. As illustrated in the transcript, the educator is active, prompting the partners to stick to their assigned listener and speaker roles, and reinforcing their positive efforts.

A common mistake is for couples to stop conversations about important topics prematurely, thinking they have understood each other when there are still unexplored and important issues. In the case of Tasha and Mark, they reported they had finished talking about where to live. I asked Mark what he meant by his earlier comment about "getting stuck in the suburban rut."

Mark: "I just do not want to live my life coming and going to work, working around the house on weekends. There should be more to life than that."

Educator: "Tasha, I am thinking this is potentially important for you to understand what Mark is driving at here. Can you ask him about what he means?"

After several minutes more conversation the educator asked Tasha what she had learned from Mark, and she said the following.

Tasha: "Mark's parents split up when he was in his late teens. He just told me that when his Dad told him that he was leaving the family, his Dad said 'I can't take this grind of living in suburbia, work all week and then work on the house all weekend.' Mark says he's really worried by the idea of getting into that same rut his father could not stand."

Educator: "So Mark wants to avoid what his father felt trapped by?"

Jana: "Yeah. He sees having a baby and giving up on living in the city, as part of .... he called it joining 'the suburban living dead'."

Tasha and Mark continued their conversation at some length at home after this session, exploring what each of them felt made up a "good life" together. They talked about the likely changes becoming parents would make to their lives, and how to keep their relationship a central priority. The transcript illustrates how, when partners really start to listen to each other important issues can emerge. In many couples important issues remain hidden and unexplored because the couple never gets beyond the initial disagreement, as in Mark and Tasha's case when they focused on their disagreement about whether to buy a house or not. The educator often can help couples to open up hidden issues by prompting the partner's curiosity in each other, and encouraging each person to keep asking questions. The educator can also look for key phrases that seem to have emotional meaning, like Mark's comment about "getting stuck in the suburban rut," and show how to open up discussion on these issues.

Conflict Management Ground Rules

Table 4.6 sets out some potential ground rules that couples might use to enhance their conflict management. The couple reads through the conflict management ground rules and tick which ground rules they currently use in their relationship, and identify ones they would like to try in their relationship in the future. A space is provided for partners to add their own suggestions for a ground rule.

When reviewing this activity with a couple it is helpful to ask them questions such as: "*Which ground rules did you each identify that you use? Thinking back into the past where and when have you managed your differences effectively – what ground rule – or structure helped you to talk constructively? If you started to escalate how could you prevent destructive conflict?*"

Table 4.6 Ground rules for conflict management

Freedom to Raise Issues Any time Either of us can bring up an issue at any time. (As distinct from trying to find a good time and place to raise issues.)	❑ Yes Time limit ______	❑ No
Right to Reschedule A partner can say, "this is not a good time." This partner should set up a time to talk soon. (You need to decide what "soon" means. Some people like to set a 24-h limit, others leave it for a little longer.)	❑ Yes	❑ No
Regular Relationship Meetings We will hold regular couple meetings when we are relaxed and alert	❑ Yes	❑ No
Under Stress, Focus On the Immediate Issue Under stress, we deal with the immediate issue on the spot, then talk about the larger relationship issue later at our couple meeting	❑ Yes	❑ No
Use of Problem Solving Sheet Sometimes we will use a written problem-solving sheet to help stay focused on the topic under discussion.	❑ Yes	❑ No
Clear Agenda We can agree sometimes to discuss just <u>one</u> issue at a relationship meeting	❑ Yes	❑ No
Understand then Solve When we are discussing a problem, we agree first listen to each other about the nature of the problem. Suggestions to solve the problem will come only after we understand each other's point of view	❑ Yes	❑ No
Use of Time Out If we start to become angry or upset either one of us can call a "time out". The partner who calls the "time out" will schedule a time soon to talk more, when he or she is feeling calmer	❑ Yes	❑ No
Use of Stop If we start to become angry or upset either one of us can call a brief "stop." This means taking a few minutes off, like a mini "time-out." The stop gives a few minutes to reflect, and to try to talk more calmly	❑ Yes	❑ No
Your Ground Rule (1):	❑ Yes	❑ No
Your Ground Rule (2):	❑ Yes	❑ No

One idea about structure is the use of a formal problem-solving approach. Table 4.7 shows the structure of problem solving in a worksheet that couples can use. Often we show couples this worksheet and explain what is involved in each of the steps. In a session with one couple it is useful to work through an example of relevance to the couple. In a group context it can be useful to identify a common problem for couples and have the group do a problem-solving exercise. For example, you could have couples discuss what level of paid work each partner will do after the birth of a first child. The group can be asked to brainstorm up a range of options, and then to identify possible advantages and disadvantages of each option.

The formal structure of problem solving is something that couples typically apply only when they are dealing with a difficult, or particularly important, decision (e.g., considering a new job or making a major purchase). In other words, it rarely

Table 4.7 Couple problem solving sheet
This problem-solving sheet can be used when you have a difficult problem to solve. First, define the problem. Then write down each partner's point of view and a "joint" point of view. The "joint" point of view is the shared view of the problem that you both agree on. It may take some discussion to come up with a "joint" point of view. Then generate some possible solutions to the problem. Next, think about the pros (positives) and cons (negatives) for each possible solution. Finally, choose the solution that best suits you as a couple

1. Define the issue (define clearly, specifically, positively):		
Partner 1's point of view:		
....		
Partner 2's point of view:		
....		
Joint point of view:		
....		
2. Possible solutions	Pros (*positives*)	Cons (*negatives*)
a.		
b.		
c.		
3. Solution decided upon:		
....		

seems appropriate to do formal problem solving when deciding what meal to select from a menu, or which television program to watch. However, some couples find the structure helpful if talking about an issue that has led to conflict in the past.

Consistent with the focus on self-change throughout the Couple CARE for Parents program, couples are encouraged to discuss and consider the suggested conflict management ground rules. As illustrated in Table 4.6 couples also are encouraged to develop their own ideas if they have good suggestions. The couples each discuss the ideas and then select those ground rules they believe might be useful for them. Implementing selected ground rules is a possible focus for a self-change plan for this unit.

Conflict Management Communication Skills

During this unit couples are asked to identify an area of disagreement in their relationship, and to hold a conversation of 4–5 min on that topic. If they have difficulty identifying a topic, they can refer to the areas of disagreement they reported on in Table 4.3. Table 4.8 sets out a conflict management communication skills self-assessment form. The identified conflict management skills build upon the communication skills already introduced, adding some skills of particular relevance to managing conflict. Couples use this form to do a self-evaluation of their communication after their discussion.

Table 4.8 Conflict skills self-evaluation form

On your own Place a tick in the box that best describes how you think you went during the discussion. (Remember, you won't necessarily use all these skills.)

0 No use of this skill
1 Some use of this skill
2 Adequate but there is room for improvement
3 Good use of this skill
N/A Skill not applicable

	Skill	0	1	2	3	N/A
Conflict skills	I listened first before offering solutions					
	I balanced listening and speaking to about equal time					
Speaker skills	Described specifics					
	Expressed positives					
	Asserted negatives					
	Self-disclosed feelings					
Listener skills	Attended					
	Encouraged					
	Summarized content					
	Paraphrased feelings					
	Asked questions					
	Reserved judgment					
Couple ground rules	Used a written problem solving sheet					
	We stayed with one agenda issue					
	We used the floor technique to control speaking and listening roles					
	We called a time out, and rescheduled the discussion					
	We called a brief stop because it got heated, then started again					
	Other ground rule (write in):					

In face-to-face sessions it is important to focus couples on the idea that the goal is to develop more effective means of conflict management. For that reason it can be useful to have each partner write down a specific goal they have for the discussion with respect to being constructive in the way they talk with their partner. It also can be useful to forewarn couples that some people find it hard to stop talking about a topic of disagreement; they tend to get caught up in wanting to make their point. It is an important skill for people to be able to break off from a discussion and return to the topic at a later stage, and this task provides the chance to practice that skill. Asking one person to act as a time keeper, and to say when 4 min are up, is a useful way to limit the discussion. As noted earlier, it is important to intervene if a couple is escalating in negativity.

After the discussion each partner completes the self-evaluation form in Table 4.8. Next, each partner should write down some feedback to give to their partner on their communication during the discussion. As in previous feedback each person identifies two positive things that their partner did during the discussion, and shares them first. Then the person offers their partner one suggestion for change. Based on their own self-evaluation and the feedback from the partner, each person should identify some areas of strength in their current communication during conflict and one area they could improve upon.

In work with a single couple the educator reviews with each partner the strengths and areas for change they identified for themselves. In a group setting the educator can have partners report back to the larger group on their strengths and areas for change. Alternatively, each person having a discussion about his or her strengths and weaknesses with another group member can be helpful. The aim is to have everyone receive reinforcement of some of their strengths as a communicator, and to have specific ideas for something to work on to enhance their communication during conflict discussions.

Recovering After a Conflict

The intention with the exercises to this point in the unit has been to make conflict management effective, and to reduce the chance of destructive conflict. Effective conflict management is likely to reduce the severity of negativity during conflict, which makes recovery easier. However, even people with very good conflict management skills, and a very strong relationship, get stressed and manage conflict poorly from time to time. Being able to recover after a negative interaction is important for all couples.

There are two parts to this exercise. First, each partner reflects on and writes down the thoughts and feelings that occur to them after a conflict with their partner. Second, the couple discusses how they currently recover after an argument or disagreement. These ideas can be introduced referring to Table 4.9, which shows some negative, unhelpful thoughts and some positive, helpful thoughts that someone might have after conflict with their partner. Words like the following can help explain the ideas. *We all have thoughts going on in our head most of the time. These thoughts can be seen as self-talk we make quietly to ourselves. Sometimes our self-talk can help us to focus and solve a problem, but other times the self-talk can be unhelpful. For example, a girlfriend might be talking about someone who had a long or difficult labor. If your self-talk was "how awful, I could not cope with that. I am scared stiff that my labor will go wrong", how might that make you feel?* [Wait for woman to answer. Ask the man about his ideas of how such thoughts would impact on him.] *What might be some helpful self-talk?*

The intent in introducing the self-talk is to explain how thoughts can influence feelings, and how the process of changing self-talk can help recovery after a conflict. Table 4.9 sets out an example of positive and negative self-talk by a man after an argument with his partner. It can be useful to go through the example and ask them what affect these thoughts might have on the man, and his likely future response to his partner. The educator could ask the couple to turn to this handout and to imagine they have just had an argument with each other and to say these thoughts to themselves. Or the educator can say the thoughts out loud as if having those thoughts. Ask the partners to talk about what effect having such thoughts might have on how they feel, and how that might influence what they say or do next

Table 4.9 Positive and negative relationship self talk example
Instructions: If you ever have an argument with each other, and across a life time together it is certain you will, then how you react after the argument is really important. Most of us have a series of thoughts, like statements we make quietly in our heads to ourselves, after something upsetting. Sometimes these self-statements are negative, they keep us focused on stoking our anger and upset. Look at the thoughts listed in the left hand column of this handout. Notice how each of these thoughts focuses on what the partner did wrong, how unfair they were, and how it includes the thinker making broad sweeping statements about the partner's negative personality, which ends with non-constructive conclusions to managing the conflict

Negative self talk	Positive self-talk
"What on earth is wrong with her! Can't she see we haven't got enough money to go spending it on take-away every day!."	"She is really struggling making dinner. She says the baby cries all afternoon and doesn't stop till after I get home. We used to get take-away a lot before she stopped work – before Emma came along."
↓	↓
"I never spend any money – she spends it all, and has nothing to show for it. I am not going to let this happen anymore!!"	"We have always been opposites: spender and a saver couple. Sometimes the difference has been a good thing."
↓	↓
"She's always been like this. She never listens to me. She has no sense"	"We had it easier in the past. This is going to be hard to adjust to a tighter budget. Maybe I need to help her with dinner. She doesn't really look like she is coping – she's been crying sometimes too, I think Emma's crying is really getting to her"
↓	↓
"We are never going to get ahead like this!!"	"I want to get our budget back into control – but we have less money now, so we have to figure out what is reasonable to spend on take-away"
↓	↓
"I would be better off without her!!"	"I love her. She might need more support. Maybe we can talk about this using the problem solving sheet – I need to figure out a time when she is looking relaxed, when the baby is not fussing or crying, and ask her if we can make a time to talk about a few options for managing dinner so that it meets both our goals."

when they see their partner. It is useful to then review the positive thoughts in the right hand column, and highlight how they focus on identifying the helpful and unhelpful things the thinker did during the conversation. It also is useful to note that calming thoughts, telling yourself to relax, and to focus upon what you can do to improve your feelings toward your partner is helpful.

Practice Tip
The focus on the "self" empowers the thinker by focusing on what she or he can change about their own behavior.

In helping people to recover better after a conflict it can be useful to ask the couple to share positive things they have done in the past to recover after conflict, and to consider ideas for what they could do differently. In a group setting it can be instructive to have couples tell the group the most helpful things they have done in the past to recover after an argument. Two points that often are useful to draw out from such a discussion are as follows. First, often people need a little time to process negative feelings, and giving each other some space after a disagreement can be useful. This does not mean storming out of the house, slamming the door and shouting "I may be back." It does mean leaving the person alone, perhaps suggesting "look we are both upset, how about we each take a little time to calm down and then let's talk about things later." Second, saying sorry and perhaps even saying that you love the person is really useful. That does not mean you are saying the other person has no responsibility for what happened. It does mean that you are expressing regret that you made a contribution that might have upset the other person, and that despite the upset, the relationship remains important. Useful suggestions for what partners could do differently to recover from conflict in the future could be a focus of a self-change plan.

Conflict Management Self-Change Plan

The unit on managing differences raises a number of ideas that partners might want to focus upon in a self-change plan. The format of the self-change plan is similar to that used in the previous unit and is included as Table 4.10. In this unit the self-change plan preferably focuses on something covered in this conflict

Table 4.10 Conflict management self-change plan

On your own pick one thing that you would like to improve conflict management that involves changing something about your behavior

1. **DESCRIBE**	2. **FOCUS**
Describe the issue you would like to work on clearly and positively …………………………………… …………………………………… …………………………………… …………………………………… ……………………………………	Describe what you currently do …………………………………… …………………………………… What are the **pluses** of your current behavior? …………………………………… What are the **minuses** of your current behavior? ……………………………………
3. **SET GOAL**	4. **EVALUATE—Afterward:**
Define exactly what I want to do. Where and when will I do it? …………………………………… …………………………………… What might get in the way? How will I make sure it happens? …………………………………… ……………………………………	What did I actually do? …………………………………… What positives resulted? …………………………………… What negatives resulted? …………………………………… What do I do from here? ……………………………………

management unit. If a partner struggles to identify a self-change plan for this unit, the educator can assist that partner explore ideas about conflict management. If that exploration suggests the partner does not have a meaningful self-change goal for conflict management, then the self-change plan can build upon previous learning, and to develop their skills in selecting self-change goals that are most likely to bring benefits to the relationship. For example, the educator should review with the partners all the ideas covered in the unit and then ask the partner to talk about the potential benefits of a self-change plan focused on any of the unit exercises. Here is an example of this process.

Educator: "We've covered quite a lot of ideas on conflict management in the session today: identifying your current patterns of conflict management; the concepts of conflict guidelines and ground rules; your communication skills when discussing conflict; and recovering should destructive conflict occur. Patrick, what thoughts do you have about a self-change plan for managing differences?"

Patrick: "I felt I did not explain myself clearly when we talked about when our child might go into child care. I have been keen for Tammy [Patrick's partner] to go back to work reasonably soon after the birth. But Tammy does not like the idea of going back to work for at least a couple of years. I tend to get annoyed about that as I see the advantages for us financially if we are both working. Deciding on child care has been a problem for us, so I am keen we get that sorted, we need to make a decision soon if we are to sort out what money we will have coming in after the birth."

Educator: "That sounds a good choice of topic, an important aspect of managing an important topic. What do you have in mind that you will do to be a better speaker?"

Patrick: "Well I want to set out what I see as the big pluses of child care for our baby and for us as a family."

Educator: "Right, so you would like to explain to Tammy that you see this as an important decision, and you want to be able to set out the key points you see in favor of your idea. And if you do that, what effect do you think that might have on how you and Tammy talk about this issue?"

Patrick: "Tammy will understand my point of view, and ...well I still don't think she will agree. So I feel we likely will still be stuck."

Educator: "Patrick, you have focused upon making sure you explain your message clearly to Tammy, but now you are saying that even if you do that it might not actually help resolve the problem. Any thoughts on what else you might do that would actually solve the problem?"

Patrick: "I think the only way it's going to get settled is if I give in."

Educator: "Really? So no matter what you say, you feel Tammy has no likelihood of changing her view?"

Patrick: "Yeah, I mean she just seems so set against our child going to child care, she wants to be home for at least two years, maybe until our son is ready for school, for reasons I just don't get."

Educator: "Interesting. So you feel you do not get why Tammy has the ideas she has. If you two are going to make a decision you both feel happy with, then each need to understand the other. I am thinking that maybe you want to do something to help you understand Tammy's views better as well as making sure she gets yours."

Patrick: "Like what?"

Educator: "Well, if you think about the listening skills we covered, any that you could try to get a better understanding of Tammy on this issue?"

Patrick: "I guess I have switched off sometimes when we talk. I do need to ask her some questions."

Educator: "That's good, a really good focus. So it seems you have two aims, first to be the listener and ask lots of questions, and secondly really attend. Then when it comes to your turn to speak you want to be clear on spelling out the advantages you see for child care and an early return to work for Tammy. Have I got it right?"

Patrick: "Mmhmm. I can do that, listen and then speak."

A common theme running through this example, and many partners' communication, is that they need prompting to listen. A useful maxim for people is: "if you wish to be understood, seek first to understand."

Managing Common Challenges in Running This Unit

Some People Struggle to Recognize the Need to Listen When Managing Conflict

It is important to help people to develop their listening skills, and to highlight for them how that can assist in reconciling after conflict. The process is illustrated below.

Educator: "Patrick, what thoughts do you have about a self-change plan for managing differences?"

Patrick: "I did not explain myself clearly when we talked about when our baby might go to child care. I am keen for him (it is a boy) to go from when he a few months old. But Tammy (Patrick's wife) does not like the whole child care thing, she wants to stay at home and care for him. We need to make a decision soon if we are to book him in."

Educator: "That sounds a good choice, an important aspect of managing an important topic. What do you have in mind that you will do to be a better speaker?"

Patrick: "Well I want to set out what I see as the big pluses of child care for us, like Tammy can get back to her career, we can keep up the mortgage payments without being really tight."

Educator: "Right, so you want to explain the key points you see in favor of your old view. And if you do that, what effect do you think that might have on how you and Tammy talk about this issue?"
Patrick: "Tammy will understand my point of view, and… well I still don't think she will agree. So I feel we likely will still be stuck."
Educator: "Patrick, you have focused upon making sure you explain your message clearly to Tammy, but now you are saying that even if you do that, it might not actually help resolve the problem. Any thoughts on what else you might do that would actually solve the problem?"
Patrick: "I think the only way it's going to get settled is if I give in."
Educator: "Really? So no matter what you say, you feel Tammy has no likelihood of changing her view?"
Patrick: "Yeah, I mean she just seems so set against child care, for reasons I just don't get."
Educator: "Interesting. I am thinking that maybe you want to do something to help you understand Tammy's views better as well as making sure she gets yours."
Patrick: "Like what?"
Educator: "Well, think about the listening skills we covered, what could you work on to get a better understanding of Tammy's view?"
Patrick: "Look I do switch off sometimes when we talk; I just feel we've been around and around this. Maybe I need to ask her some questions."
Educator: "That's a really good focus. So you have two aims, first to listen and ask lots of questions, and really attend to the answers. Second when you speak to be clear on the advantages you see for child care. Have I got it right?"
Patrick: "Mmm-hmm. I can do that, listen and then speak."

A common theme running through this example, and many couples' communication, is that they need prompting to listen. Patrick is like many other people who imagine that if they can just find the right words, then their spouse will change their mind. But of course the spouse is also likely to be convinced that they have the right solution. Unless each person listens to the other, things do not change. A useful maxim for people is: "If you wish to be understood, seek first to understand." In this example, despite his resolution, Patrick did not listen to Tammy. The educator broke in and praised him for his clarity of speaking but asked if he had done any listening. He acknowledged that he had not, so the educator had the couple use a piece of paper as the floor and gave it to Tammy. Even then, Patrick kept disagreeing with Tammy's comments. The educator broke in for a second time and modeled for Patrick how to listen actively to Tammy. One issue that Tammy mentioned was her concern that quality child care was hard to find. She also worried about how well she would manage returning to work in the first few months after the birth. This issue had not previously been broached and Patrick got interested in that issue. This particular example illustrates an important issue—that sometimes the educator needs to use a variety of strategies to help people develop their listening skills, particularly when they are discussing things that are important to them.

The Couple Tries to Solve the Problem Prematurely

A second challenge, which often co-occurs with not listening enough, is that people begin a discussion about differences by suggesting a solution. This inhibits a full discussion of each person's view. This was evident in Patrick and Tammy's discussion. Tammy began the discussion by saying, "I think I should stay home to look after our baby. The money I might make by going back to work will be chewed up by child care fees." The educator pointed out that she had started with the solution before either partner had described what they thought were the important issues. The educator asked Tammy to start again but this time to talk about some of the things she wanted to see in the care arrangements for her son. A thorough exploration of each partner's perspective on key issues provides the basis on which a couple can generate a mutually acceptable solution.

The Couple Escalates to Arguing

It is important that the educator structure the session to provide a safe opportunity for the couple to discuss difficult topics, and to reduce the chance of a heated argument. If couples argue in front of an educator they often feel embarrassed, it erodes their motivation to continue, and might lead the couple to drop out of the program. It is important for the educator to create the setting such that the chance of escalation is reduced, to model being pleasant and polite, and to make it clear that civility is expected of all participants toward each other. In addition, the task of discussing a conflict topic needs thorough preparation. This includes making sure people have a clear understanding of the various conflict management strategies covered in the unit, structuring the discussion task so that people are focused on positive strategies they are trying to employ.

If the couple does escalate their disagreement, the educator needs to intervene quickly. That means asking the couple to pause. If one partner is particularly angry, it is best to work with that person first. Ask the other spouse to listen without interrupting and indicate you will speak to them about their experience of the interaction soon. Explore with the first partner how they are feeling and be empathic. The following is an example of the process.

Diana: (angry, raised voice) "Brian, that's rubbish. You never want to visit my parents."

Brian: (derisively) "Hah, you mean you never notice all the time we spend over there."

Educator: "I want to stop you there folks. Diana you seem angry, and Brian you don't look very comfortable either."

Diana: "Well, Brian frustrates the hell out of me. He just won't agree to visit my parents. We see his father almost every week, and yet going to see my folks is always a big deal!"

Educator: (turning to Brian) "It seems things are not going well in the discussion."

Brian: "No, Diana is getting emotional, again."

Educator: "OK, look, all three of us need to understand what is happening here. Brian, I want to ask for your help. I want you just to listen for a few minutes while I speak to Diana. I want you to remain quiet and really listen. Once Diana has had a chance to explain her point of view, I will ask you to say in your own words how she sees things. You don't have to agree with what Diana is about to say, but I do want you to try to understand her. OK? Will you do that?"

Brian: "OK."

Educator: "Diana the floor is yours. Please tell me how you were feeling in the discussion with Brian."

Diana: "I get so frustrated. I feel we go over this time and time again. We both work long hours. We both value our free time. But I finish up visiting his father but never seeing my mother. It's just not reasonable."

Educator: "OK, so you see Brian spending time with his father, but as not doing his fair share to make sure you see your parents. Is that it?"

Diana: "Yeah, we have the discussion. And like just now Brian denies, he says, 'What about how I went over there for dinner Thursday night?' Yeah, he did but I have not seen my mother for four weeks before that. We spent last weekend staying at his Dad's place, and cooked for him Tuesday and Wednesday. I even did the shopping, for the food we cooked."

Educator: "And when you point out what you see as the unfairness, what happens?"

Diana: "He argues the point with me. He comes up with an odd visit here or there."

Educator: "So it sounds like you two get into a debate about how often you see each of your parents, and your big point – that you feel that Brian does not support your desire to see your parents."

Diana: "Exactly."

Educator: "And you're frustrated and angry that a similar conversation keeps happening?"

Diana: "Absolutely, I am really fed up with this."

At this point the educator notices Diana's anger is abating a little. He checks that he has really understood and then asks Brian to summarize Diana's viewpoint. Then the educator talks to Brian about his experience of the discussion. In this instance both partners agreed that the discussion was a recurrent problem. The usual pattern was that Diana would start the conversation with a complaint; Brian would become defensive and argue back, the discussion would escalate with a focus on each person debating their contribution and usually Brian would withdraw. The educator talked to them about ways to overcome this pattern of approach and withdraw, and suggested they try the floor technique.

This example illustrates the importance of the structure of listening empathically to one partner at a time. We recommend starting with whoever seems the most upset, as it is often more challenging for them to listen to the partner. Through the exploration of the discussion we try to identify the process of what is going on, how the person feels, and something of their views on the topic at hand. Being empathically listened to usually helps people to manage their negative feelings. Moreover, calm interjections from the educator often help to interrupt the escalation, and then the educator can then steer the couple toward different possible ways of approaching the conversation.

In essence, the pervasive challenge in helping couples manage differences is to create a safe environment in which each person feels comfortable to express themselves. Some couple therapists reading this might question the wisdom of exploring difficult issues in a group context. However, doing CRE is different to couple therapy. Most of the time the couples undertaking CRE can discuss differences without escalating to destructive conflict. Nonetheless relationship educators do need to monitor how effectively couples undertaking CRE are managing conflict, and be ready to assist couples that lapse into destructive conflict.

Moving Toward the Birth

On the completion of this unit the couple have completed exercises to clarify their expectations about managing the transition to parenthood, and their social support needs. The couple have been assisted to develop their communication and conflict management skills through education, reflection, and self-change. We recommend doing a follow-up with the couple (usually a brief telephone call of 10–12 min) a week or so after the current session to check on completion of the self-change plan. The next scheduled session for the couple is after the birth, and focuses on managing the challenges of infant care. We usually do this as a home visit, and will check in with the couple a week or so after the scheduled birth to set up a time for that session.

Chapter 5
Taking Baby Home

Chapter Highlights

This chapter describes how to do the following:

- Debrief the birth experience to help the couple develop a shared understanding of this important life event.
- Review key infant care tasks, discuss baby care, and sensitive and responsive parenting which guide the couple to develop a shared parenting approach.
- Discuss the good and challenging things about parenthood, and review how the partners support one another.
- Identify and challenge negative parenting self-talk, and help parents develop positive parenting self-talk.

This chapter describes a unit of Couple CARE for Parents designed to be delivered in the first few weeks after the birth of the couple's child. These first weeks are usually very busy and some couples struggle to settle into a regular routine, so the major focus is on assisting couples manage the challenges of infant care, develop individual stress management skills, and mutual support to manage the high demands of infant care. The content and activities of this unit are summarized in Table 5.1. Typically it takes about 1.5–2 h to cover the content and activities, although this can take longer if the baby is fractious. Although Unit 3 can be offered in a variety of ways, we recommend delivering this unit in the couple's home. A home visit is often helpful to the couple as it can be hard for them to attend sessions elsewhere during the early days of parenting. The visit enables the educator to see the home environment and discuss how the couple are coping, and supporting each other. Almost all of the work of this unit can be completed during the home visit.

Electronic Supplementary Material: The online version of this chapter (doi:10.1007/978-1-4939-1613-9_5) contains supplementary material, which is available to authorized users.

W.K. Halford et al., *Clinical Guide to Helping New Parents*,
Springer Series on Couples and Health, DOI 10.1007/978-1-4939-1613-9_5

Table 5.1 Content and activities for taking baby home

Topic and aim	Tasks	Example activity
Debrief to develop a shared understanding of experiences	Explore similarities and differences in the birth stories	Open discussion and paraphrasing
Clarify expectations	Developing a shared parenting approach Educator provides information on main areas of baby care (e.g., good enough parenting) Sensitive and responsive parenting	Who is doing what? Exploring infant care needs Playing and your baby's responses
Support needs	Review concepts of emotional, problem-solving, and practical support. Plan for additional support needs	Identifying support needs and potential support people
Stress management	Self-talk	Identifying and challenging negative self-talk

The educator should aim to have the couple develop one or two specific actions to help them manage parenthood effectively. To that end, as in the previous unit, educators help each partner develop a self-change plan focused on a key area that really makes a difference to relationship.

Practice Tip
Before conducting home visits to a household with a young baby it is useful to discuss expectations with the couple. We suggest educators explain that the session takes approximately 1.5–2 h, and to use the time efficiently it is important that the couple be able to focus on the session. That means selecting a time when the baby is often settled. However, young babies are unpredictable and if the baby is unsettled it does give the educator the chance to observe how the partners manage this and to coach the partners on sensitive-responsive parenting, mutual support and stress management if required. In addition, we remind couples of the following ground rules discussed before the antenatal home visit: no television or other distractions, switch off cell phones, and choose space in the house with chairs and a table (or desk). For safety we have educators ring about 30 min ahead of schedule, check that both partners are home, and ask for any dogs in the home to be secured. It is also a good idea for the educator to let someone else (a supervisor or colleague, preferably) know where you are (address; phone number) and how long you will be.

The two units that come after this current unit can be delivered using flexible delivery in which the couple complete activities at home, and the educator reviews the content with the couple by telephone or internet video-conference. The self-directed learning materials couples need to do the exercises are described at the end of this chapter. Often we give these to the couple at the end of the current session.

Alternatively, these materials can be mailed (or emailed) to the couple a week or so before the next scheduled session.

After the birth couples are often very keen to discuss their birth experience. There are a number of benefits from talking about the birth, including developing the relationship between the couple and the educator as well as debriefing any trauma experienced during the birth. Hence in this chapter we discuss strategies to facilitate a discussion about the birth. A key goal of the content in this chapter is to help couples develop a shared parenting approach; develop sensitive and responsive parenting and good stress management strategies.

Debriefing the Birth Experience

Introducing a debriefing discussion about the birth is usually fairly easy as most couples welcome the opportunity to talk about the recent experience. In fact, when we first started offering Couple CARE for Parents, we had not planned to debrief the birth experience. However, we found almost all couples wanted to discuss the birth, and there proved to be benefits from having this discussion. To start the conversation is often as simple as asking "*How did it go*?" For some couples, a slightly more detailed invitation to speak is useful.

There are many different responses when describing the birth, such as "great," "better than I expected," "long," or "painful." Some births are experienced as predominantly very positive, but not all births go as planned, and some women who experienced a distressing birth may be forthright and say, "I found it really traumatic," "awful," "a nightmare." Other women may be less forthcoming about their distress in comments that indicate the birth was survival of an ordeal and may say something like, "At least the baby is fine" or "At least I didn't have a caesarean" or "Fine, I had to have a caesarean but it's OK." These responses could alert the educator that not all is well and further discussion is warranted.

Given it is the mother who gives birth; it is perhaps understandable for the birth to most often be a more psychologically impactful experience for mothers than fathers. For example, if the mother had hoped for a natural birth with relatively few drugs or medical intervention, then needing medication or having a surgical delivery (i.e., caesarean section) can prompt the woman to think that she is "failure" as a mother. In contrast, her partner may simply be relieved that both mother and baby are fine. At the same time, some fathers report feeling overwhelmed by witnessing the demands of labor and its effects on their partner. Both mothers and fathers often benefit from the opportunity to talk through their experiences, fears, and concerns. The educator needs to be sensitive to possible variations in responses, and provide empathy to both parents.

In most cases the birth is perceived as a joyous, if testing, occasion and after 10–15 min of sharing, the couple are able to move on to other content in the unit. However, in about 5–10 % of births the woman may experience some significant stress reaction from the birth. This stress reaction can range from mild, but still distressing stress symptoms, through to a diagnosable post-traumatic stress disorder. Severe stress reactions are characterized by intrusive thoughts and images about the birth (possibly including nightmares); anxiety when discussing or thinking about the birth and a desire to avoid reminders of the birth; negative alterations in mood and thoughts after the birth; and increased arousal or reactivity. It is much less common for men than women to experience these sorts of stress reactions to the birth, but such problems do sometimes occur in men.

If, in the process of birth debriefing with the couple, it becomes apparent that one or both partners need to talk through a distressing birth in greater detail, then a separate session could be offered face-to-face or over the phone. Trauma-induced stress responses usually decrease with time. For example, it is very common for people to have high physical and psychological arousal immediately after experiencing a trauma, whether that trauma is a car accident, an assault, or a difficult birth. Across a period of days and weeks the arousal usually declines. Clinical post-traumatic stress disorder (PTSD) can be thought of as a delay in resolution of the stress symptoms. If a parent experiences stress symptoms that are severe, or do not seem to decline with time, then the educator might recommend the couple contact a psychologist or other counseling service to seek further assistance.

Practice Tip
Childbirth can be extraordinarily stressful and overwhelming. Relatively few women (less than 15 %) report that maternity staff asked how they felt about the birth. Debriefing after the birth may be the first occasion offered to many couples to discuss their experiences.

After discussing and summarizing the birth experience, focus the couple's attention on how they are managing the demands of parenting and how they are supporting each other. It is useful to ask the couple to reflect on the content covered in the previous units (that are usually conducted before the birth) on parenting expectations, support needs, communication, and conflict management. We usually ask each partner to write down one or two ideas they liked from these earlier units, and how these ideas have been used in their relationship. The couple can then discuss together what they wrote down. This also allows the educator to check what the couple have remembered, and to remind them of the content that has been covered.

Sensitive and Responsive Parenting

After discussing the birth, the remaining goals of Unit 3 are to encourage sensitive and responsive parenting; promote couple confidence and competence to offer adequate baby care; and foster mutual support and positive self-talk. The educator may introduce this content by saying, "*The first weeks after the birth of the baby are usually very busy. I'm interested in knowing how each of you is managing the demands of parenting and how you are supporting each other. Almost all of the work of Unit 3 is completed during this home visit. By the end I hope you each will identify at least one or two actions you want to take that will assist you manage parenthood even better than you are now.*"

At this point the educator can introduce the couple to the notion of "good enough" parenting. The educator might say something like, "*There is no right way to be a parent. Parenthood constantly changes as your child develops. All couples will have bad days and good days with parenting. Your baby does not need you to be a perfect parent, but they do need you to be a good-enough parent.*"

There are five areas in which parents need to provide "good enough" parenting. The first area of providing for the basic needs of the baby involves providing warmth, shelter, food, rest, hygiene, and protection from danger. Second, a baby requires affection which the couple gives through holding, cuddling, kissing, and admiring their baby. The third area is playing with and stimulating your baby. The fourth involves stability and providing a calm routine. The final area involves responding sensitively to the needs of the baby.

Clinical Connection
What are some examples of good parenting of a young baby that you have done, or seen done by others? What are some common errors couples make in the first few weeks after taking their baby home?

It is important to recognize that flexibility is often needed in the approach couples take in caring for their newborn infant. Couples often find the plans they had for parenthood have to be modified once the baby arrives. For example, the mother might intend to return to work a few weeks after the birth, but have a difficult birth and not feel able to return to work when originally planned. Even seemingly small decisions made before the birth might need to be rethought. For example, couples might plan to have their baby sleep in their bedroom or might set up a separate nursery. Some couples who have their baby sleep in their bedroom find the baby's night time noises and wakening disturbs the sleep of both parents. Other parents find having their baby sleep in another room is anxiety provoking as they feel unsure whether they will hear if their baby is unsettled. There is no one right way to manage these decisions, and the couple need to be encouraged to discuss the pluses and minuses of their options and try to find the best option for them as a family.

Couples can access a vast amount of information on becoming parents. For example, many first-time parents attend antenatal classes. Many new parents read books or consult internet sites for parenting advice. Most get some parenting advice from health professionals like pediatricians or nurses, particularly advice related to health outcomes such as eating and sleeping routines. Almost all new parents all receive advice from some mixture of grandparents, friends, and work colleagues. Many new parents find it hard to integrate the sometimes conflicting advice they receive about parenting. For example, parents are variously advised to follow a schedule for breast feeding or to feed on demand; to sleep their baby in the parental bed or not; and to swaddle a newborn in a wrap or not. In Couple CARE for Parents we encourage partners to discuss parenting with professionals and others, as support and advice can often be useful. At the same time, ultimately it is up to the couple to make decisions that best suit them and their baby.

Practice Tip
Well intentioned advice from family and friends sometimes helps new parents, but sometimes can be confusing. The educator helps by reviewing the advice received and having the couple discuss what they find valuable in the advice. This discussion can be complemented with information provided by the educator, with the ultimate aim that the partners to develop a shared approach to how they choose to parent.

There is now a substantial body of research on infant care. Much of this research shows that there is a range of ways key parenting tasks can be undertaken that are consistent with raising a healthy baby. However, some advice might not be optimal. We routinely ask couples about the advice they have gotten about parenting, and what they have found useful. Such a conversation is helpful to clarify the support the couple is receiving and provide opportunities to correct misconceptions. Such a conversation could be initiated by questions like the following. "*What is the most helpful parenting tip you have received? What advice have you been given that you did not think was a good idea, and why was that advice not right for you?*"

Baby Care

When a couple first bring their baby home, they often are surprised at how fragile and small their baby seems. They will quickly find that the baby probably sleeps a lot and cries a bit (or a lot!). Some new parents find it hard to know what to do with a baby. The basic task of infancy is to *develop trust.* The educator might introduce this idea with the following words. "*Like all babies, your baby is relying on adults around them to make sure they are safe and comfortable. When parents are 'good enough parents' they provide the baby with what the baby needs (food, comfort) and are responsive to the baby, and this helps the baby develop trust in you – a sense that they are safe. You can encourage your young baby to develop trust in you and be happy by:*

- *responding appropriately to your baby's physical needs*
- *providing a safe environment*
- *showing affection*
- *spending time with your baby when they are calm*
- *encouraging eye contact and talking gently*

- *carrying them (a baby sling is a great way to keep their baby close and leave the parent's hands free)*
- *reducing noise, light and distraction when your baby is tired or distressed*"

Educators can ask partners to describe a time when they did something to build their baby's trust in them, and explore how their baby reacted to this.

Bonding with Baby

Bonding is the emotional attachment—"falling in love"—that occurs between a parent and baby. Some parents bond with their baby at birth. Other parents take longer to form this bond. There is no right or wrong time for new parents to develop a bond with their baby, but parents who have a close bond with their baby tend to be more sensitive and responsive to their baby. Helping partners identify ways they bond with their baby is a key way educators can help each partner provide good-enough parenting.

Clinical Connection
Think of a time when you were with a young infant and felt close to that baby. (It might be your own child, or the child of a friend or family member.) What were you doing when you felt close to that baby? What is the experience of a new parent like in those special times with their own baby?

One activity to promote parent–baby bonding is to ask each partner to complete the handout titled "*Playing with your baby*" (see Table 5.2) which describes how to be a sensitive and responsive parent while spending time with their baby. Each partner is able to tick off the games/activities which they have already tried with their baby, and note how they perceived the baby reacted to them.

Practice Tip
Babies are born with a number of features that help bonding. Sharing information with parents and asking them to reflect on their baby's abilities can encourage a deeper appreciation of their baby's attributes. For example, it is worth pointing out the following facts:

- Babies' vision is best when they are held between 7 and 9 in. from their parent's face, usually the distance between a mother and her infant when breast feeding.
- Babies' hearing is tuned into human voices and they prefer voices over other sounds.
- Babies have different cries which parents will learn to recognize as signals for hunger, or distress or tiredness.

Table 5.2 Playing and your baby's responses
Tick off the games which you have already tried with your baby. What was your baby's reaction?

Games	√, I have tried this	My baby's reaction …
Touch *Giving your baby lots of cuddles and kisses *Stroking and massaging your baby *Playing kissing and raspberry games *Rhythmically playing bicycles with your baby's legs *Rest your baby on your chest, skin to skin *Letting her touch objects with different textures		
Hearing *Playing rhythmical music (nursery rhymes and lullabies) *Singing to your baby *Talking to your baby in a high pitched tone with lots of variation *Cooing to your baby—take turns making the cooing noises *Commenting on the things your baby is looking at		
Sight Babies prefer to look at faces. Face games may include: *Adult pokes tongue in and out and waits for baby to copy. Adult copies infants mouth movements *Smiling at you baby when she/he looks at you is a great way to form a loving bond *Look into her eyes and keep loving eye-contact *Babies also see black, red and white better than other colors. Show your baby toys made in these colors		
Smell *Give your baby new sweet things to smell—e.g., a scarf that smells like mum, a t-shirt that smells like Dad, a flower from the garden (make sure it has not got too much pollen), or take baby into the kitchen when you are cooking and comment on the smells		
Balance *Games that involve balance—e.g., rock, gently swing or dance with your baby *Once your baby has some control over her head gently bounce her on your knee *Say "up, up, up" and gently move your baby up into the air (support your baby's head and shoulders)		

The educator should take the opportunity during the home visit to observe the couple with their baby, watch to see how comfortable each partner is with their baby, and how they talk to their baby. Ask each partner what they see as their strengths as a carer for the baby, and what they see as the challenges they face as a carer. As the couple talks, watch for whether there seems to be tension between the couple when caring for their baby or when discussing their care of the baby. Through discussion the educator can provide suggestions to parents based on the points made above as practice tips. For example, if a parent holds the baby very close when looking at the baby's face (less than 6 in. or 15 cm away) or too far away (more than a foot or 30 cm distance) it makes it hard for the baby to focus and see the parent's face clearly. The educator's role in reviewing parent knowledge and coaching is to enhance parenting competence, and help the couple be a team in their approach to parenting their baby.

Practice Tip
The secret of couples adopting potentially helpful advice is timing. It is important that the couple be active and asked how to address parenting challenges. Suggestions are best offered when the couple is stuck and wants to hear a suggestion.

In addition to play and bonding with the baby, parents need to perform the key infant care tasks of sleep, feeding (including breastfeeding), and attending to crying. These areas can be sources of stress for a parent, and between partners. The handout in Table 5.3 can be used to assist parents self-evaluate their infant care in each of these key tasks. Ask each partner to write down their answers in the spaces provided and then have the couple discuss together their thoughts. The Couple CARE for Parents approach is to encourage the couple to observe and problem-solve together to reach a mutually acceptable approach to parenting, using the educator as a resource for prompting discussion, coaching and offering suggestions if the couple seeks information or advice.

Table 5.3 Handout for parents to review baby sleep and feeding

Sleep
Describe your baby's sleep–wake behavior..
....
What is going well with baby's sleeping behavior? ....
....
Are there any aspects of baby's sleeping that you are concerned about? ....
....
What support do you have for managing sleep problems from your partner, your close family and friends? ....
....
Feeding
How is feeding going? ....
What is going well? ....
Are there any aspects of feeding that you are concerned about? ....
....
What will I/we do to improve feeding? (write your ideas down here) ....
....
What support do you (the mother) have for breastfeeding from your partner, your close family and friends? ....
....

Sleeping

As noted in Chap. 1, soon after birth infants' sleep patterns are haphazard, with sleep occurring in relatively short bursts (typically from 2 to 4 h) across the day and night (Teng et al., 2012). When awakened, newborns usually require feeding or parental soothing (Sadeh, 1996), and the consistent caregiving means fatigue is almost universal among parents of young infants (Sinai & Tikotzky, 2012). About 30 % of parents report sleep disturbances in their infants (Teng et al., 2012), and for them the fatigue can be very debilitating.

Across the first year of life most infants gradually increase their longest sustained period of sleep from the 2 to 4 h typical of newborns to around 7–8 h (Henderson, France, & Blampied, 2011). The largest increases in sleep duration tend to happen across the first 1 to 4 months of life, with more gradual increases in maximum sleep duration after that (Henderson, France, Owen, & Blampied, 2010). Infants also learn to sleep more at night and less during the day, which results in about 60 % of infants sleeping through the night (continuously asleep from 10 pm to 6 am) by around 12 months of age (Henderson et al., 2010).

These above basic facts can be summarized to parents to help them develop realistic expectations of the development of diurnal (day–night cycle) regulated sleep. It is useful to ask parents about how their baby is sleeping, and to estimate the longest duration of their sleep, and the extent of night-time sleeping. It also can be useful to ask about how baby's sleep has been changing across time. You might then relate their statements to the normative data summarized in the preceding two paragraphs. That explanation could go something like this. "*You say that now Alice is two weeks old she is sleeping 2 to 3 hours at time, and typically wakes at least twice during the night. That sounds a very typical pattern in these early stages. We would expect her to gradually move toward sleeping 7 to 8 hours at night across this first year. She also will gradually sleep a bit less during the day and more at night.*"

For parents who are concerned about their baby's sleeping, there are a number of tips that can be offered that assist infants to learn to sleep for longer, and to sleep more at night. Specifically, the following points based on a review of the research by France, Blampied, and Hnederson (2003) are worth reviewing with parents and seeing what they do relative to these tips.

1. Provide clear cues as to whether it is day or night such as low light at night, brighter lights in the day, and less activity at night than during the day. This helps the baby to learn to discriminate night and day.
2. Look for signs of tiredness such as yawning and grizzling and use them to signal that the baby needs to sleep.
3. As often as possible place the baby in the crib awake so she or he is learning to go to sleep in that place.
4. Recognize that babies need to learn to self-soothe, and allow them time to settle after being put down to sleep. Avoid rushing in and picking them up, giving lots

of attention, or stimulating them (turning on lights, talking) if the baby does not settle right away.

5. If the baby has had the chance to settle but remains restless, then use soothing strategies (e.g., gentle speaking, rubbing back slowly).
6. Pay attention to your baby's behavior when she or he is unsettled and try to learn to identify the state of your baby. When babies dream they will often move about, can open their eyes and close them, and even call out. Most times if they show some passing disturbance associated with dreaming they will, if not disturbed, settle back to sleep. In contrast when babies are truly awake they open their eyes fully, look around, and that suggests they are active and alert. If it is daytime this is the time to engage with them. If the baby is active and alert during the night-time use strategies listed here to help the baby settle and return to sleep.
7. Try to carry out stimulating activities (playing, bathing, changing, and feeding) at particular times that are distinct from when you want the baby to sleep. In the lead up to sleep time try to use low stimulation activities, reduce noise, light, and use gentle speaking and physical touch to relax your baby.
8. If you have to carry out feeding or diaper changing at night try to do it in dim light, with little noise, minimal talking, and minimal stimulation.

There is a lot of variability in how infants develop their sleep patterns across the first year of life. Some infants are just more challenging than others to manage, and parents of such infants might need considerable support to develop good practice to assist develop their baby's sleep. About 20 % of infants show continuing difficulties with learning sleep patterns and at about 6 months or so, planned ignoring might be introduced. However, this is not recommended for infants under 6 months of age. Further guidance on managing infant sleep problems in children older than 6 months can be found in France et al. (2003).

Practice Tip
Some parents can be understandably very concerned about their baby's sleep, but also might have concerns about some tips offered. In particular, some parents worry about the idea of not immediately responding to their baby when their baby is unsettled. It is important to emphasize that you are not recommending planned ignoring, or leaving the baby for a long period of time. Rather you are suggesting the baby be allowed time to settle. It is fine for parents to quickly check if a fussy baby is safe, but that checking should not involve arousing activity (e.g., talking, picking up baby). A highly distressed baby does need soothing (see tips on managing infant crying). Prompt the parents to reflect on any concerns they have about any suggestions you offer, demonstrating empathy with those concerns, allowing the couple to choose which strategies they would like to try as well as discussing how to implement the ideas is important.

Breast Feeding

Many women will want to breastfeed their baby for a period of time. The World Health Organisation recommends that babies be exclusively breastfed until 6 months of age (American Academy of Pediatrics, 2012). Most working women find it challenging to sustain exclusive breastfeeding for this period of time. The support of the father is important to assist the mother to commence and sustain breast feeding if that is her choice. Consequently, the couple might want to discuss ways to enable the woman to continue morning or evening breast feeds for as long as possible. If the woman chooses to breastfeed, the following tips can be useful to review and discuss with the couple.

A common problem associated with breastfeeding relates to how the baby attaches to the breast. The baby needs to have a wide-open mouth to get as much breast tissue into its mouth as possible whereas most people incorrectly believe that the baby obtains milk by sucking on the nipple only. To demonstrate this you could ask the couple to suck on the end of their finger and suck as if they were sucking on a nipple. Ask the couple to think about the shape of their mouth, cheeks and jaw, and how they feel. Now, ask the couple to open their mouth wide and suck on their arm. Once again ask them to notice the shape of their mouth, cheeks and jaw. Some useful discussion points the educator can use to review this exercise are as follows. "*What was the difference between the two types of sucking? What do you think would happen when a baby is nipple sucking as opposed to breast suckling? What would happen to the nipple? Which method would allow the baby get the most milk?*"

Feeding on Demand

Another useful concept is breastfeeding according to need, often referred to as feeding on demand. Feeding on demand helps establish good milk supply when the infant is newborn. The educator could point out to the mother, "*You will likely have already noticed changes to the feeding patterns of your baby since the birth. Similarly, you probably have noticed changes to your breasts since giving birth. By week 3 your breasts are settling to the demands of breastfeeding and are softer. The brain, breast and baby work as a team in successful breastfeeding so a softer breast a few weeks into breastfeeding is normal. When your baby suckles at the breast then your milk flows.*"

Sufficient Milk

During the early weeks after birth, some mothers worry that they are not providing enough breast milk for their baby. However, the breasts are almost always able to supply sufficient milk for their baby—the principle of supply and demand. As the baby grows, their needs change. If there is a lack of breast stimulation, milk flow and production is reduced. Mothers can increase their milk supply by feeding more. Within 24–48 h of frequent feeding, breasts will usually produce more milk. A well-drained breast is able to produce more milk for the next feed.

Crying and Soothing

A crying baby is rated as particularly stressful by new parents. If the crying baby is easy to settle then the couple is more likely to feel confident as parents. However, even the most placid babies sometimes do not settle easily. Sometimes a baby can become really distressed. At such times the baby's face often goes red, their arms and legs are drawn up as if in pain, and the parent feels like nothing seems to work to soothe the baby. A severely distressed baby happens to almost all parents at times. It is important the couple stay calm, because distressed parents promote more distress in a baby. It can be useful to suggest to parents who report severe distress when their baby cries that they take three long, slow deep breaths—breathing out fully with each breath, and move slowly when they are becoming upset themselves. The capacity to slow down, and to be calm in voice tone and movements can help soothe a distressed baby (and the distressed parent as well). When both parents are present, it can be useful for one to do the caring while the other takes a short break. Alternating short bursts of care giving with a really distressed baby can make things seem more manageable. Another means by which parents can keep calm is by having a sense of what they can do. The following checklist in Table 5.4 can be a useful

Table 5.4 Handout for parents to review possible reasons for baby crying

Is our baby too hot or too cold?
– Check room temperature and appropriateness of clothing and any wrap
– Feel baby's skin and check for cool skin or sweating
Does our baby want to feed?
– How long is since the last time baby fed? Did baby feed well then?
Has our baby been over-stimulated?
– How long since baby last slept?
– Has baby been awake more than is usual today
Is our baby tired?
Is our baby bored and wanting attention?
Is our baby ill? Some signs of possible illness are as follows
– Has our baby developed a high-pitched cry in the last day or few hours?
– Has our baby been pooing and weeing normally?
– Has our baby become lethargic, less responsive, and reluctant to feed?
If the couple has concerns as to whether their baby is ill, they should seek medical advice

handout to provide to couples. Parents soon learn the checklist and can run through it when their baby is distressed to see if there is anything else they can do to soothe their baby.

Sometimes a baby's crying can be related to unexplained gut pains often labeled as colic or reflux. If the baby is otherwise well, and is settled at least some of the time, colic is just part of the baby's normal behavior. However, severe and unremitting colic might indicate a more serious problem and consultation with a doctor would be advisable.

If a couple are worried about their baby's crying, the educator might ask the couple to discuss the following questions. "*Do you think your baby cries more, less or the same amount as other babies? What do you do when your baby cries? When your baby is very upset what works really well to calm your baby? What seems to make your baby cry even more?*" Discussion around these questions allows the educator to provide information on typical levels of crying in young babies, and explore with the couple whether their baby is unusual in the level of crying.

If the parents are still concerned about infant crying, or you, as the educator are worried about the infant crying, it is helpful to refer the parents for more help. A useful suggestion is to take their baby to a child health nurse, or family doctor for a check-up and to discuss management of infant crying.

Parenting and Mutual Partner Support

Mutual support by the partners is important in assisting the couple adapt to parenthood. As we described in Chap. 1, research shows women who feel supported by their partners report coping better with the demands of parenthood, and participate in more affectionate and companionate activities with their male partner. Men supported by their partners report greater couple relationship satisfaction, and provide more care for their young infants. Furthermore, men's greater involvement in childcare and household tasks is related to more sensitive parenting, which in turn predicts both partners' sustained relationship satisfaction. However, if only mothers are highly involved with the infant, and a distant father–infant relationship exists, then fathers often report feeling rejected, resulting in lower relationship satisfaction for both partners. Thus, mutual support is associated with reduced parental burden and stress, enhanced couple interaction, and sensitive, engaged parenting by both partners. A guided discussion can encourage the couple to reflect on their perceptions of parenthood, and their support of each other, as illustrated below.

Educator: "What stands out in your mind Enrico, as the best thing about becoming a father?"

Enrico: "The quiet times are really special, lying in Saturday morning with little Carmen between us …. she was cooing …. and I just wanted the three of us to be there, nowhere else."

Educator: "Sounds beautiful, tranquil."

Enrico: "You know, I don't think I ever felt quite so alive, content, till I became a father."

Educator*:* "Wow, so being a Dad is a really major change in your feeling about life, you really feel alive. Noi, what is Enrico saying about his experience of fatherhood?"

Noi: "Well, he loves Saturday morning and the closeness and I do too, you know. And I love the closeness of breast feeding. If only I was not so exhausted all the time. It's the broken sleep, a few hours here, a few hours there. And Carmen, when she cries, I … really struggle sometimes, you know … it gets too much for me."

Educator: "So Noi there are some great moments you three share as a family, but you are feeling really tired, and it gets too much—especially when Carmen is upset and crying."

Noi: "I never thought it would be so hard. Maybe I am not doing this whole motherhood thing right, I feel helpless sometimes when Carmen won't stop crying."

As Noi describes her experiences of motherhood she discloses her sense of being overwhelmed, particularly by tiredness and feeling powerless to comfort her crying baby. An initial goal of the process of exploration and shared discussion is to help each partner understand the experience of the other. To facilitate this shared understanding the educator then prompted Enrico to reflect on what Noi had said. His response reflects a common challenge partners have as they seek to support each other.

Educator: "Enrico, Noi shared your enjoyment of those quiet times, the closeness with your daughter. But what else is she saying?"

Enrico: "Aah, she is tired? …."

Educator: "Right, and ?"

Enrico: "Like it gets too much? I am not sure."

Educator: "Let's see if we can better understand Noi's feelings about motherhood. I heard Noi say something about her responses to Carmen crying, and about how she is managing as a Mum. How about you ask her about these issues? What I would like you to do is to listen really carefully, and then see if you can summarize what she says. OK?"

Enrico (nods): "So Noi what is it you were saying about when Carmen cries?"

Noi: "Some days when she cries, when you are working late and I am alone, I just feel I can't manage, not on my own …"

Enrico: "Yeah but you know we both agreed I need to do the extra hours, we need the money …"

Educator: "Enrico, I want to stop you there. You have raised a potentially important issue about money, but remember your role right now is to listen. So I want you to focus back on what Noi is saying about her experience. Noi: can you tell Enrico what makes it hard when you are alone".

This passage illustrates how the educator needs to be active, and coach the partners to really listen carefully to each other. When Enrico started talking instead of listening, the educator paused and redirected the conversation. A really important function the educator has is to ensure that each parent is able to express themselves, and to be understood by their partner. If a couple is struggling to listen to each other effectively, it can be helpful to prompt them to use the speaker–listener floor exercise described in Chap. 3.

The above discussion encourages the couple to identify the things they each find good, and the things they each find stressful about parenthood. The couple could then be asked to each reflect on what they are doing to help their partner, what their partner does for them, and one or two new things they could do to support their partner. The educator could then ask the couple to discuss their answers. Useful questions to guide this exploration include the following. "*How are you supporting your partner in their parenting role? What other things could you do to support your partner? Are there things your partner could do to support you that you think would be helpful?*"

Parenting Stress Management

New parents typically experience diverse emotional reactions to becoming a parent. There often are feelings of great joy and tenderness toward the baby, and an increased sense of closeness and belonging with the partner. At the same time, almost all new parents experience some anxiety about how to parent, the adequacy of their parenting, and the effect of parenthood on their relationship with their partner.

When talking to couples about their views of parenthood the educator should listen carefully to any words expressing how each of the partners evaluates their own coping with parenthood. For example, some parents say they are reveling in being parents, while others hint at themselves being "bad parents" because they cannot stop their baby crying. Follow up on these descriptions by asking each partner for more details on their views of their parenting. For example, you might ask "*When you say you are a bad parent, what do you mean by that?*" This exploration of how the partners perceive their parenting often provides insight into their thoughts about themselves as a parent, which is considered more in the exercise that follows on self-talk about parenting.

Negative and Positive Self-Talk

The thoughts people have about parenthood can usefully be described as self-talk, a silent dialog happening inside the person's head. Some of this self-talk is negative and unhelpful and some is positive and helpful. Table 5.5 sets out a sequence of negative self-talk that might occur when a baby is crying and hard to soothe, and a sequence of positive self-talk in the same situation.

Table 5.5 Positive and negative self-talk about parenting

Negative self-talk	Positive self-talk
Focuses on what is going wrong, unrealistic, exaggerates how bad thing are, focuses and builds on negative feelings	Acknowledges what is going wrong but is realistic, soothes negative feelings, focuses on what can be done, active problem-solving approach
"There's something seriously wrong for this much crying to be happening. No baby should wail like this!"	*"A couple of hours crying every day can be normal. Sometimes babies get tired or upset and take a while to settle."*
↓	↓
"My baby cries all the time, all the time. Nothing I do stops this! Its awful, I can't stand the screaming!"	*"This crying is stressing. It makes me feel like it'll never end. But I know she really doesn't cry all the time."*
↓	↓
"I can't stop my baby crying. I'm a bad parent. I have no idea what to do. I should never have had a child, I am just not cut out for this."	*"OK, take it slow. Double check all the likely reasons for her crying. OK, I've fed her, it's a comfortable temperature. Anything in her cot making her uncomfortable. No."*
↓	↓
"I can't stand this anymore!! I have to get away. Make her stop, anything, make her stop."	*"Her nappy is dry and clean, so it's not that. Maybe she's overstimulated? I could keep holding her or maybe leaving her will help us both."*
↓	↓
"I hate this baby!!"	*"Holding her is making me tense, and that won't help her settle. OK, slow deep breath. Relax. I will turn out the light, gently rub her back for a couple of minutes until the crying softens and then leave her to see if she falls asleep."*

As the example illustrates, negative self-talk is unrealistic, focuses on and exaggerates what is going wrong, and builds up negative feelings. This negative self-talk can set up a cycle that makes the problem much worse. Babies are sensitive to the emotions of their parents, they can tell from voice tones, facial expressions and actions of their parent that the parent is upset. The baby is very likely to become more upset if the parent is upset. This sets up what is called an escalation trap: the more the baby is upset, the more upset the parent becomes, the more upset the baby becomes, the more upset the parent becomes, and so on.

In contrast to negative self-talk, positive and helpful self-talk is characterized by a realistic appraisal of what is happening, by calming negative emotions, and by focusing on what can be done. Positive and helpful self-talk soothes negative feelings (e.g. "take a slow deep breath," "do things slowly, no need to stress"), and actively problem solves about positive options. Positive self-talk helps people to respond constructively to stressful situations.

In order to help couples use more positive and helpful self-talk to manage parenting stress, it can be useful to show Table 5.5 as a handout. The educator should explain the ideas of negative and unhelpful versus positive and helpful self-talk. It can be useful to ask one of the partners to imagine being in the situation of their baby being distressed and have them read out loud the negative self-talk, and then have them describe how it makes them feel saying those negative thoughts. Then have the same partner read out the positive thoughts, asking them to read slowly and calmly. Again, ask the person to describe the effect on them of reading those thoughts out loud. Many people report experiencing strong emotions when doing this exercise, which can be a compelling demonstration of the effects of self-talk.

Practice Tip

Some parents become so frustrated and angry in response to a crying baby that they are at risk of doing something dangerous, like hitting or shaking their baby. Babies are easily injured. The baby's brain is so fragile that even shaking a baby once can result in delayed physical and mental development, or even death. It is very important to talk with parents and highlight that when really stressed parents sometimes do things they really regret later. If they ever feel really stressed when caring for their baby, and fear they might lose control, they should do three things.

1. PLACE THE BABY SOMEWHERE SAFE AND WALK AWAY FROM THE BABY.
2. Take a break.
3. Call someone for help.

Developing Positive Self-Talk

When a couple take the time to develop their own individual positive self-talk, and to support each other in the use of that positive self-talk, they will be more confident and happy parents. In order to assist partners to challenge negative and unhelpful self-talk and build positive self-talk, each person is asked to think about an event that has been stressful for them in the last week. We use Table 5.6 as a handout. In step 1, each person is asked to briefly write a description of the stressful situation. In step 2, each person writes the self-talk that they used in that situation, and then identifies what of their self-talk is positive by placing a tick in the third column. In step 3, any negative self-talk is reviewed. The person is assisted by the educator and their partner to write positive self-talk that could be used as an alternative to the negative self-talk that occurred in that situation.

The couple is also asked to complete a take home assignment to practice developing positive self-talk. During the next week each person is asked at the end of the day to reflect back on the time when they felt most stressed, and complete the handout included as Table 5.7. The person uses the first column to write down a description of the situation, and the second to write in their self-talk. They then read through

Table 5.6 Developing positive self-talk
Step 1 Describe Stressful Situation
Step 2 Identify Negative Self-Talk
On your own, pick an event that has been stressful for you in the last week. Briefly write a description of the situation, focusing on what was stressful and write the self-talk that you used in that situation in the space below

Situation	Self-talk	Positive? (√)
Example: *Middle of the night, baby was not feeding, kept pulling off the breast*	*OK, third feed for the night.* *I am so tired, I just have to get this done and get some sleep.* *This is awful, I just cannot get her to suckle.*	√
....	....	
....	....	
....	....	
....	....	
....	....	
....	....	
....	....	
....	....	
....	....	
....	....	
....	....	

Step 3 Generate Positive Self-Talk

With your educator and partner's help write helpful self-talk that could be used in that situation

New helpful self-talk
Example: *I am tired. Ok need to be calm to soothe baby, so slow deep breaths Tell myself "relax" as I breathe out. Baby is still pulling off the breast. Why might that be? Is she/comfortable? Not too hot or cold? No bright lights in the eyes? Head and baby supported? Maybe just thirsty not hungry? Still not sure, lie back relax, enjoy closeness, see if baby drifts off to sleep or tries again to feed*
....
....
....
....
....
....

their self-talk and place a tick "√" next to any self-talk that they think is positive. For any self-talk that is negative, the person is asked to generate alternative positive self-talk and write that in the final column. In a final step, the couple read each other's self-talk form and discuss the content. Each partner should try to understand exactly how the other felt in the stressful situations and what self-talk they used. Each person can gently suggest positive self-talk for the other to use when stressed.

Table 5.7 Developing positive self-talk as a habit
During the next week, at the end of each day write down the situation when you felt most stressed that day. In the first column write the situation, and in the second write in your self-talk. Place a tick "√" next to any self-talk that you think is positive. For any negative self-talk write down alternative positive self-talk in the fourth column

Situation	My self-talk	Positive? (√)	Positive self-talk
………………………	………………………		………………………
………………………	………………………		………………………
………………………	………………………		………………………
………………………	………………………		………………………
………………………	………………………		………………………
………………………	………………………		………………………
………………………	………………………		………………………
………………………	………………………		………………………

Discussions about stress and negative self-talk are intended to build couple awareness of each other's stress and to assist them to provide support to each other with these stresses. The self-talk monitoring and challenging activity is reviewed with the educator during the telephone call that is part of the next unit.

Self-Change in Adapting to Parenthood

The final activity in this unit asks each person to reflect on the material that has been covered in the unit, pick one thing they wish to change, and write a self-change plan on the form provided in Table 5.8. Some examples of self-change plans that some participants have developed when doing Couple CARE for Parents include: using breathing or muscle relaxation to calm oneself when stressed by a crying baby; adapting how the baby is placed on the breast to encourage wide mouth attachment to the breast; the father getting up and bringing the baby to the mother for night-time feeds; the couple setting aside time to have a cup of tea together in the morning at least once per week to discuss how they are managing; one parent trying at least two of the baby play and bonding activities introduced in this unit; the father arranging to take some part-time holidays and work part-time for a couple of weeks to share the parenting load.

The educator should state they will review the implementation of the self-change plan in the next session. It can be very helpful to frame the self-change plan as an experiment. The person tries the self-selected change, and then reports on whether that change was implemented and if so what effect the change had.

Table 5.8 My self-change plan
On your own pick one area in your relationship that we have discussed in this unit and you would like to improve. Choose an area that is important to you. Follow the four steps below

1. **DESCRIBE**	2. **FOCUS**
Describe the issue you would like to work on clearly and positively …………………………………… …………………………………… …………………………………… …………………………………… ……………………………………	Describe what you currently do …………………………………… …………………………………… What are the pluses of your current behavior? …………………………………… What are the minuses of your current behavior? ……………………………………
3. **SET GOAL**	4. **EVALUATE—Afterward:**
Define exactly what I want to do. Where and when will I do it? …………………………………… …………………………………… What might get in the way? How will I make sure it happens? …………………………………… ……………………………………	What did I actually do? …………………………………… What positives resulted? …………………………………… What negatives resulted? …………………………………… What do I do from here? ……………………………………

Managing Common Challenges in Running This Unit

The Couple Finds It Hard to Make the Time To Do Couple CARE for Parents Around the Demands of Infant Care

In our experience most couples complete all, or almost all, of the program. At the same time, it is not unusual for couples to report tiredness ranging through to exhaustion in the early weeks of looking after a newborn baby. Many of our couples will ask to reschedule a session if they are particularly tired, which is common if the baby has been ill or not slept well. Flexibility in allowing rescheduling is important. At the same time, we do ask couples to negotiate the time and date of the next session. Some couples suggest they will contact when they are ready, but we find that approach impractical when managing staff workloads.

We deliberately designed the CCP program so that the first unit after the birth has no demands on the couple outside the session. We also focus the content of the session on issues most often salient to couples caring for a newborn. This makes sustaining couple engagement more likely. Furthermore, the flexible delivery options of Couple CARE for Parents enable the educator to remain in touch with the couple in a diversity of ways (by phone, email, or face-to-face) without the couple needing to travel.

We also want to emphasize that the educator should feel free to modify the content of the unit to suit the needs of the couple. For example, it could be that following a distressing birth, the couple has a strong need to talk through the birth in detail and develop a way forward in terms of understanding what happened during the labor and birth. Alternatively, if there are problems with a particular aspect of infant care (e.g., breast feeding, crying) then the focus can be on those challenges. The emphasis should be on content salient to the couple, while still retaining the emphasis on mutual partner support and managing stress being integrated into discussions.

Practice Tip

In our experience there is a need to balance flexibility with a degree of structure around how couples engage with the program. An advantage of flexible delivery is the capacity to reschedule if a couple have a lot of competing demands on their time at a particular point in time. However, couples seem to benefit from regular contact with the educator to enhance engagement and motivation to continue, and the content of each unit reflects the challenges couples often experience at particular times after the birth. We recommend to couples that they complete one unit of the post birth program each month, and ask couples to advise us at least 24 h ahead if they wish to reschedule a session.

There is an Imbalance in Parenting Skills Between the Partners

In the first months after birth the mother usually assumes a larger proportion of childcare than the father. This is partly determined by biological realities, like only the woman can breast feed. The gender difference in parenting also reflects that, in most Western countries, there is greater provision for maternity leave than paternity leave. One common effect of this gender imbalance in parenting is that mothers develop parenting competency faster than fathers. We often note to new parents that babies train up their parents, and the parent that gets the most training from their baby is often more competent. This can result in the father feeling less competent, which can be exacerbated if the mother is critical of her male partner's parenting. ("*No, that's not right, let me do it.*") In such situations, it is easy to understand how a father may feel discouraged and withdraw somewhat from parenting. Mothers might then feel a sense of burden in doing more and more of the parenting.

It can be useful to highlight the risk that a couple can inadvertently fall into very traditional gender roles of infant care. If the couple agree they want to adopt such traditional roles, then that is fine. However, many couples want to share the parenting roles. Participation in Couple CARE for Parents aims to help couples have the best relationship they can, and to make considered decisions. Hence, reviewing the sharing of infant care and whether the partners are happy with the current balance is a useful exercise.

One Parent is Clinically Distressed

The period after the birth of child is the highest risk time of any through the life cycle for women to develop depression, and there is elevated risk of anxiety disorders as well. There also is elevated risk of depression for fathers. Educators might well be the first professionals to detect clinical depression. If a parent reports sad mood, it is worth discussing how long that mood has persisted. If it has persisted for a few weeks or more then referral to a doctor for assessment is indicated. Some people might be reluctant to seek help. One useful strategy is to ask them to complete the Edinburgh Postnatal Depression Scale (Cox, Holden, & Sagovsky, 1987), which is a 10-item measure of depression. The scale is in the public domain and can be downloaded from http://www.blackdoginstitute.org.au/docs/cliniciansdownloadableedinburgh.pdf. In addition to giving a score indicating the likelihood of clinical depression, discussing the person's answers provides an opportunity for the educator to clarify the person's experiences and be empathic. Such a process makes it more likely the person will accept the referral.

Preparing for Flexible Delivery of Couple CARE for Parents Units

In the usual way we deliver Couple Care for Parents (CCP), as set out in Table 1.1, the last three units of CCP are provided in flexible delivery mode. That involves the couple completing a series of tasks, both individual and joint tasks, prior to a session with the educator. The tasks are described in a series of handouts that the couple works through, which introduce key ideas, ask the couple to discuss these ideas relative to their own relationship, and then apply at least one idea in a self-change plans. The session with the educator reviews the couple's work together, and the review session is conducted by telephone or by Internet video-conference.

In order for couples to complete the tasks, the handouts need to be provided to the couple ahead of time. Educators might choose to provide these handouts and explain the flexible delivery system at the end of the current unit, and hence we include this note on the need to prepare for flexible delivery at the end of this chapter. At the beginning of Chap. 6, we describe in more detail how we implement flexible delivery of the last three units of CCP.

Chapter 6
Sharing Infant Care

Chapter Highlights

This chapter describes how to do the following:

- Provide the program in a flexible delivery format.
- Help couples analyze their current patterns of time use, and promote a healthy balance of individual, couple and family activities.
- Revise roles and pre-birth expectations to enable couples to negotiate a shared approach to parenthood.
- Help couples identify their social support needs.
- Help each partner develop a self-change plan to implement an idea based on this unit.

This chapter describes specific strategies for couples to review their current balance of time use in individual, couple, and family activities; and whether they are happy with that balance. They also discuss their current sharing of household, parenting, and other family roles; and negotiate a shared approach to managing parenthood. The couple considers the support they offer to each other, and receive from others. As with most other units, the final activity involves developing a self-change plan to apply the unit's learning to the couple's own relationship.

The content, activities, and associated handouts for this unit are summarized in Table 6.1. Typically the unit is offered around 6–7 weeks after the birth of the baby. As noted at the end of the previous chapter, this unit is usually provided in flexible delivery, which involves the couples completing the activities described in the handouts in their own time. The activities take about 1 h for couples to complete. They then have a

---

Electronic Supplementary Material: The online version of this chapter (doi:10.1007/978-1-4939-1613-9_6) contains supplementary material, which is available to authorized users.

W.K. Halford et al., *Clinical Guide to Helping New Parents*,
Springer Series on Couples and Health, DOI 10.1007/978-1-4939-1613-9_6

Table 6.1 Content and activities for your time and tasks

Topic and aim	Tasks	Example activity
Review of Unit 3	What stands out in your mind as the most important part of the last unit which covered parenting, baby care, and dealing with stress	
Achieving a happy life balance	Explore perceptions of parenting	Open discussion and paraphrasing
Satisfactory distribution of chores and baby care	Explore how the couple shares the tasks of newborn care Document actual chore/care demands	24 h clock of infant care demands in a typical day
Enhancing support	Explore support needs of each partner	Who is doing what? Exploring infant care needs
Support needs and change plan	Review concepts of emotional, problem solving, and practical support. Plan for additional support needs	Identifying support needs and potential support people

review session with the educator that typically takes 45–50 min to complete. Thus the total time commitment for the couples to complete the unit is about 2 h. The final two units of Couple CARE for Parents, which are described in Chaps. 7 and 8, are also usually provided in flexible delivery format, and each takes about 2 h of couple time.

You might prefer to provide this unit of Couple CARE for parents, or all of the remaining three units, in face-to-face sessions. If so, then go through the exercises with the couple(s) guiding them.

Practical Issues in Flexible Delivery of Couple Care for Parents

Flexible delivery has a number of advantages for couples. First, it allows couples to complete all of the remainder of the program from their home, and to do most of the activities at times that suit them. It also has the partners do these things as a couple, which promotes generalization of the learning after the program is finished and the educator is no longer supporting the couple. At the same time the review sessions provide some educator support to the couple in completing the unit.

Flexible delivery also has a number of advantages for professionals delivering programs. As the couple does much of the work before the review session with the educator, the educator's time can be used efficiently. Conducting the review sessions by telephone or Internet video-conference eliminates travel time associated with home visits, yet still allows the couples the convenience of not having to travel to participate in a session with the educator.

Despite its advantages, flexible delivery is not necessarily appropriate for all couples. It is likely that at least some couples prefer face-to-face rather than flexible delivery. Nonetheless, we obtain a very positive response to flexible delivery of couple relationship education from the vast majority of couples. Couples complete an average of nearly 95 % of all the recommended activities, drop-out rates tend to be low, and high consumer satisfaction with the program is reported (Petch et al., 2012; Wilson & Halford, 2008). However, couples with low levels of formal education do drop out more than other couples from flexible delivery (Petch et al., 2012), which probably reflects them struggling with the reading required in flexible delivery mode. (Although new parents couples with low education also drop out more frequently than other couples from relationship education offered in face-to-face sessions (Halford & Petch, 2010).) We have found that working through the materials with couples via telephone or Internet videoconference can be helpful to couples who have low levels of formal education. This obviously takes more time than the couple working through the materials themselves, so we use this option selectively.

Making Flexible Delivery Effective

Couples need the materials about a week ahead of the scheduled review session. This allows the couple to have sufficient time to complete the tasks, but is not so far in advance of the review session that the materials are likely to get mislaid. It is important to note that EACH partner needs a copy of the handouts, as there are some activities done individually and some activities done jointly. The relevant materials appear in this chapter as Tables 6.2, 6.3, 6.4, 6.5, and 6.6, inclusive. A single booklet entitled A Couple Guide to Sharing Infant Care, which includes all these handouts,

Table 6.2 My current activities

On your own: Fill in the following boxes on activities you have done since the birth of your baby

Individual activities without your partner or baby …………………………………… …………………………………… ……………………………………
Couple activities (just you and your partner) …………………………………… …………………………………… ……………………………………
Individual or couple activities with your baby …………………………………… …………………………………… ……………………………………
Shared activities with your partner, baby, and others (family, friends) …………………………………… …………………………………… ……………………

What are the major changes in your pattern of time use since the birth of your baby? Write your thoughts in the box below. Then discuss these changes with your partner
Changes in how we spend our time
…………………………………… …………………………………… …………………………………… ……………………………………

Table 6.3 On your own: how do you feel about your current mix of activities?
On your own tick the boxes that apply to you

❑ I would like more <u>independent</u> activities ❑ I would like fewer <u>independent</u> activities ❑ I would like some new <u>independent</u> activities ❑ I am happy with my <u>independent</u> activities as they are, no changes are needed
❑ I would like more activities with my <u>baby</u> ❑ I would like fewer activities with my <u>baby</u> ❑ I would like some new activities with my <u>baby</u> ❑ I am happy with my <u>baby</u> activities, no changes are needed
❑ I would like more <u>couple</u> activities with my partner ❑ I would like fewer <u>couple</u> activities with my partner ❑ I would like some new <u>couple</u> activities with my partner ❑ I am happy with our <u>couple</u> activities, no changes are needed
❑ I would like more <u>shared</u> activities with my partner and others ❑ I would like fewer <u>shared</u> activities with my partner and others ❑ I would like some new <u>shared</u> activities with my partner and others ❑ I am happy with my shared activities, no changes are needed

As a couple discuss your answers to the above exercise which looks at how happy each of you are with the current mix of activities. Your educator will discuss these activities during the telephone call for this unit

Table 6.4 Reviewing the sharing of household chores and infant care

Step 1. Review your pre-birth expectations of childcare and household chores
Turn back to the division of labor table that you filled out in the workshop. With your partner discuss how your pre-birth expectations are similar or different to what is happening now. Don't try to change anything yet, just discuss the similarities and differences
Step 2. Evaluate the current distribution of household and child care tasks
On your own, write down some things you are happy with, and anything you want to change in the division of household chores and child care The things I am happy with ……………………………………………………………………………………….. ……………………………………………………………………………………….. ……………………………………………………………………………………….. The things I would like to change ……………………………………………………………………………………….. ……………………………………………………………………………………….. ………………………………………………………………………………………..
Step 3. Discuss your answers and identify any areas to be negotiated
Share your answers from the previous two questions. At this point do not try to make any changes, just seek to understand your partner's viewpoint, explain your own viewpoint, and write down in the box below the tasks which you each want to change as a couple Child care and household tasks for us to review ……………………………………………………………………………………….. ……………………………………………………………………………………….. ………………………………………………………………………………………..

(continued)

Table 6.4 (continued)

Step 4. Get ready to discuss possible changes
Before you discuss these topics further complete the following a. Write down a communication/conflict management skill you will use when discussing this topic with your partner. (Choose a communication skill which will improve the success of the discussion). Remember to use your speaker and listener skills when talking with your partner. Use problem solving if you both get stuck on negotiating a better way to divide the work (a sample problem solving sheet appears as Table 4.7 in Chapter 4) The communication/conflict management skill I will practice = …………………………………………………………………………………….. ……………………………………………………………………………………..
Step 5. (Negotiating about changes) is done in the review session with educator

Table 6.5 Reviewing your support needs
Write down in the box below who is giving you support in your new role as a parent, and what is the most helpful aspect of the support they are providing

Support person	Most helpful thing(s) this person does to support me
Partner………………… ………………………… …………………………………………………… Others: (name them) ………………………………………………….. …………………………..	…………………………………………… …………………………………………… …………………………………………… …………………………………………….. …………………………………………… …………………………………………… ……………………………………………

Is there any other type of support you think you need? On your own identify some strategies for obtaining this support. Discuss with your partner your support needs and also ask about your partner's support needs

Additional support I need	Strategies for getting the support I need
…………………………………………………… …………………………………………………… …………………………………………………… …………………………… …………………………………………………… ……………………………………………………	…………………………………………… …………………………………………… …………………………………………… …………………………………………… …………………………………………… …………………………………………… ……………………………………………

can be downloaded from the Springer link web site for this book at http://link.springer.com/chapter/10.1007/978-1-4939-1613-9_6. These materials are available for you to reproduce and use in your professional work. You might give the couple the handouts at the end of the previous session, but make sure you ask them to name somewhere in their home where the materials can be safely stored. Alternatively, you might mail or email the booklet to the couple a week or so before the scheduled review session.

About a week before a review session is due we ring the couple, briefly check in how they are going, check they have the unit materials at hand, and confirm the date and time for the review session. We restate it is important for the couple to set aside

Table 6.6 A self-change plan for unit

On your own pick one thing reviewed in this unit in your relationship that you would like to improve. Choose an area that is important to you

1. **DESCRIBE**	2. **FOCUS**
Choose an issue you'd like to work on that involves changing something about your behavior. Describe this aspect clearly and positively (write in the spaces provided) .... ______________________________	What do I currently do? .... What are the **pluses** of my current behavior? .... What are the **minuses** of my current behavior? ....
3. **SET GOAL—Define exactly what I want to do**	4. **EVALUATE—Afterwards:**
Where and when will I do it? .... What might get in the way? How will I make sure it happens?	What did I actually do? .... What positives resulted? .... What negatives resulted? .... What do I do from here? ....

an hour to complete the activities in the materials provided. We usually send a text message reminding the couple of the appointment 24 h ahead.

When you provide the materials to the couple it is important to explain the content to be covered, and give the rationale for what that content is potentially important. The explanation could be something like the following. "*These materials cover four key areas. First, almost every couple finds that how they spend their time changes a lot after having a baby. So our first activity is to have you review your current balance of time use, how that has been affected by becoming a parent, and whether you are happy with that balance. It is important, as far as is practical, to have some time for yourself, some for you as a couple, and time with your baby. We can talk in our next session about how parents might sustain quality couple time and the importance of this for relationship satisfaction. Second, you review your current sharing of household, parenting, and other family roles; and negotiate a shared approach to managing parenthood. You also will be asked to consider the support you offer to each other, and receive from others. The final activity involves developing a self-change plan to apply the ideas covered in a way that you think makes sense for your relationship.*"

As this unit is the first time flexible delivery that has been used in the Couple CARE for Parents program, it is helpful to give a brief explanation of how this system works. "*The idea is that there are activities in which you are asked to write down what is going on for you two, and then discuss your answers. Each of you gets a copy of the materials so you each write in the spaces provided. It usually takes people about 50 to 60 minutes to work through these tasks. Then I call you at the agreed upon time and talk to both of you about your answers, and I will help out with anything you might want to explore further. I also will review the self-change plan you wrote at the end of the last unit. What questions have you got about any of that?*"

It is useful to discuss some guidelines for making the review sessions at the end of this unit and subsequent units effective. First, it is important that the educator can speak to both partners simultaneously, and that the educator and the partners can all hear each other. A telephone with a speaker is suitable, but a telephone without speaker is not. An Internet video-conference can work fine (e.g., Skype), provided the couple has an external microphone and speakers on their computer. A computer with a headphone is not suitable for conducting the review session. Discuss with the couple what options they have available. If possible a video-conference is preferable, as that provides extra nonverbal cues about partner's reactions to the tasks. However, we have delivered CCP very successfully with only audio contact.

Aside from negotiating the communication technology to be used, many of the guidelines for conducting the flexible delivery session are the same as for the home visits. Both partners need to be available for the whole session. The session needs to be conducted somewhere quiet, free from distractions (turn off television and cell phones for the review session), and which offers the couple privacy.

We ask couples that, if they need to reschedule for some reason, to please give us notice at least 24 h ahead of the scheduled session. Notice can be provided by telephone or email in our system. If couples do reschedule we contact them within 48 h to renegotiate an alternative time.

At the start of the review session it is important to remind the couple of the agenda. This consists of reviewing their implementation of each partner's self-change plan from the previous unit, and reviewing the activities they undertook in this unit. It is important to check with the couple that they have actually completed the activities. (We discuss what to do if they have not completed the activities in the section on *Managing Common Challenges in Running this Unit* later in this chapter.) Also ask the couple to have their completed guidebook materials in front of them. We also like to remind the couple that the session will take about 45–50 min, and to check they are both available for that time.

Reviewing the Taking Baby Home Self-Change Plan

In the previous unit of Couple CARE for Parents the couple reviewed how they were managing the challenges of caring for a new born (bonding with the baby, and managing infant sleeping, crying, and feeding). At the start of the review session it is helpful first to ask the couple about what they remember of what was covered in the previous unit. Questions might be of the following form. *What do you remember of what we covered when I visited you at home after the birth of your baby? Is there anything in particular that you found valuable in what was covered? Have you used any of the ideas we discussed since then?*

The educator should then ask each partner about how they went with their self-change plan. The process followed is as for previous reviews of self-change plans. Specifically, the following questions are useful to explore. "*How did you go with the self-change plan? Can you tell me exactly what you tried to do? On a scale from 0 to 10 (with 0 being "did not do anything like I planned" to 10 "completed exactly what I intended") how well would you rate your carrying through of your self-change plan?*" If the person did as they planned, then the following questions are useful: "*What benefit, if any, was there for your relationship or your partner from you doing this? What else do you plan to do to follow up on this?*" If the person did not complete the plan, then use the three-step process described in Chap. 4 to problem solve how to implement the self-change plan effectively.

The other activity covered in Chap. 5 (Unit 3) was identifying and challenging negative and unhelpful thoughts. Educators should ask each partner if they have completed the self-talk self-monitoring form (Table 5.7), if they caught themselves thinking any negative self-talk in the past few weeks, if they shared the negative and unhelpful self-talk with their partner, how they challenged or reframed the thought, and how they felt after challenging it.

Exploring Patterns of Time Use

The first activity of Unit 4 is a review of patterns of time use. Before the review session with the educator the partners were asked to list the activities they currently undertake using the form presented in Table 6.2, and then review their satisfaction with their balance of individual, parenting and couple activities using the form presented in Table 6.3. Before asking the couple about their answers it is useful to briefly restate the rationale for focusing on this issue. You might use words like the following: "*As you now know, having a baby changes how you spend your time. The change is quite dramatic, isn't it?*" After responding to some initial comments from the couple, the educator could continue with, "*Understandably couples often have less time to talk to each other, and less time for fun, because of the demands of infant care. Getting away from the house to visit friends, let alone plan a weekend away, can now be much harder. Many new parents find they get very little "me time", or couple time. Over time, in a healthy relationship the couple balances the time they spend doing things individually, the time they spend doing things together as a couple, the time they spend with their children, and the time they share as a couple with other people. There is no one correct balance. Each couple needs to find the balance that suits them. The balance changes around as well, particularly around the needs of children. At this time of major change in your lives together, it can be really useful to reflect on the current balance of your time, how it's changed after the birth of your baby, and whether you want to fine tune that time use.*"

Clinical Connection
Think about the balance of activities in your own life. How has this changed over the last 5 years? What has influenced those changes? What are the positives and negatives of these changes for you? Are there some changes you would like to make to your balance of activities? What are some barriers to any change you might want to make? How could you overcome these barriers? How might you use these reflections to assist couples you are working with?

The educator should discuss with the couple the different activities that make up their use of time. This includes their individual interests, time together, time with the baby, and time shared with others. Some possible dialog to introduce this topic could go something like the following:

"We each need individual interests to develop our own unique selves. No two people have exactly the same interests. Maintaining individual interests and hobbies brings new ideas and experiences into your relationship. Time together with just the two of you heightens your sense of closeness. It allows you to have fun together that are just between the two of you. It provides special time to communicate privately as a couple. Time with your baby is important. Both time you spend one-on-one with your baby and time you spend as a couple with your baby. Shared activities with others, such as extended family and friends, bring fun and variety into your lives. It helps builds a network of people outside your relationship who can be there for you."

"If the balance of individual, couple, baby-focused, and shared activities does not feel right, problems can develop. Parents who have too little time for themselves as an individual report they often feel a loss of their sense of self. They may have little interesting to say to their partner, because there is nothing new or interesting happening. Couples who have very little couple time often feel a loss of intimacy. They may find it hard to get the chance to talk to each other about issues that are concerning them. Couples with few joint activities shared with others may feel cut off as a couple from friends and extended family."

In this review session the educator asks each person about their answers to their form presented in Table 6.2. It is useful to follow up with a question along the following lines. *How has your time use changed since the birth of your baby? What are the best aspects of these changes?* (Here we might prompt for positive time with the baby, both one-on-one and with their partner, if the couple does not mention this.) *What are the aspects of these changes that are hardest for you?* The educator could ask the couple, or summarize for the couple, how the changes in time use after having their baby are perceived as similar or different by the partners.

The educator should ask each partner then to describe their answers to the questions on their level of satisfaction with their balance of individual, parenting and couple activities (using the form in Table 6.3). The process of review enables each partner to clarify their feelings about their current mix of activities, and express any desires for change. The educator can then prompt the couple to discuss how they could support each other to try to get the balance of activities they desire.

Practice Tip
It is helpful to frame the review of current activities as an opportunity for the couple to understand how being a parent is affecting each of them in terms of what they get to do. Having some time to focus on themselves as individuals, and some time for them as a couple, is important to help them sustain a mutually satisfying relationship.

It is useful when discussing the review of the couples' balance of individual, parenting and couple activities, to remind couples of the desirability of allocating at least some couple time. Some new parents see couple time as very difficult to maintain in these early months of their child's life. It can be worthwhile to explore with these couples what holds them back from scheduling time for the couple relationship. A common error is to focus on doing what they did as a couple before parenthood (e.g., going out for dinner at night), and for many new parent couples they see that as unrealistic, and conclude any couple time is too hard to arrange. What couples do with their time together tends to evolve across time, and the need for flexibility when becoming parents is particularly important. Sometimes half an hour together having a cup of tea and listening to each other, having a picnic in the backyard (or on the balcony), or just giving the partner a foot rub, can be a vital affirmation of the importance of the couple relationship. It can be useful to ask the couples what they think will happen in the long term if they do not make time for couple focused activities now. Helping the couple develop a strategy for setting aside time specifically for the couple relationship, even if couple time is brief, is important.

Sharing of Parenting and Household Tasks

The next part of the session reviews how the couple shares the division of labor in their relationship. A lack of shared, realistic expectations concerning the division of labor can lead to resentment and conflict. Often couples assume more traditional gender roles after the birth of the child than they had previously. Traditional gender roles develop for a combination of reasons, including the following: (1) The biological-based reality is that the woman needs to recover after child birth and usually needs at least some time off work for that recovery; (2) Only the woman can breast feed and with the frequent feeding needs of an infant she will often need to be in caring for the baby in order to be able to breastfeed on demand. (3) In many countries parental leave for mothers is more widely available than is parental leave for fathers, which means she is often at home caring for the baby, while the father returns to work. These three reasons can increase the pressure for the mother to assume more of the responsibilities for childcare and household tasks. In many couples women report that they feel parenting ultimately is primarily their responsibility.

Almost by default the father assumes primary responsibility for financially supporting the family. For some fathers they devote more of their time to paid work after the birth of their first child than before becoming a father, because they feel final responsibility for finances and for financially supporting their family. Many couples find themselves adopting these traditional roles despite a desire to be more egalitarian in their role divisions.

There can be advantages to traditional gender roles, such as clear understanding of which partner completes which work roles. For example, in a traditional family, the mother will attend to the baby crying; the mother will do the food shopping and prepare meals, and not expect the father to do these tasks. Further, the male will go to work each day, earn the money, and not expect the women to do paid work. The adoption of traditional gender roles after birth works for some couples, and for couples who expect and embrace this approach to gender role, there is likely to be fewer conflicts about "who does what." On the flip side, a disadvantage of traditional roles is that couples can lose a sense of understanding about each other's world. Women can end up feeling disappointed, tired and alone in their parenting; while men are often stressed about money, feel that they have no leisure time, and that their life is no longer any fun.

Many modern couples have lived an egalitarian lifestyle before becoming parents and if either partner expects an egalitarian division of labor in the early months of parenthood but experiences a traditional division of labor there is likely to be dissatisfaction and some negotiation required. For example, women who want egalitarian gender roles can be very dissatisfied if their partner adopts a traditional gender role and does not "do his share" of household and parenting responsibilities.

This unit provides an opportunity for couples to review their division of tasks and is an opportunity for couples to examine the similarities and differences between pre-birth expectations and post-birth reality. The main aim of this review is to allow couples who are unhappy with the division of labor to negotiate a more satisfactory division of labor now, early in parenthood, in a structured and low-threatening format. For couples who tend to show poor conflict management patterns this activity can prevent the build-up of resentment. If a couple reported earlier in the Couple CARE for Parents program that they have difficulty with conflict management, then the educator can play a particularly important role in helping the couple negotiate parenting roles constructively.

Practice Tip

Before doing the current review session it is useful for educators to review their notes on the couple's conflict management. In particular, check if the couple reported use of the escalation, demand-withdraw, or avoid patterns of conflict management. If so, remind the couples of the unhelpful pattern of conflict management they reported using, and ask each partner to nominate one thing they will do to be constructive in their discussion of parenting and household tasks in this review session.

As part of the self-directed activities done in preparation for the review session, couples are asked to review changes in their household and parenting tasks by referring back to the division of labor table that they filled out in the pre-birth workshop. A handout of this four step activity is presented in Handout 6.4. Couples are asked to do the following: (1) Review the pre-birth expectations of childcare and household chores. (2) Evaluate the current distribution of household and child care tasks by each partner and write down some things they are happy with, and anything they want to change in the division of household chores and child care. (3) The couple discusses their answers and identify any areas to be negotiated. At this point the couple is not asked to agree on changes, just seek to understand their partner's viewpoint, explain their own viewpoint, and write down the issues to be negotiated. (4) The couple considers how to approach negotiation of solutions. Each partner writes down a communication/conflict management skill they will use when discussing this topic with their partner. (The couple should be encouraged to choose a communication skill which will improve the success of the discussion.) The couple might use problem solving if they have got stuck negotiating a better way to divide the work.

By following the four-step process described above the couple should then be ready to discuss and negotiate any issues about distribution of chores in the review session with the educator. Moreover, each partner should also be able to nominate one thing they will focus upon to try to make the discussion productive. In the review session the educator plays an important role in keeping the couple on task, ensuring each partner is listening to the other. Please note: in the activities completed at home couples are encouraged to discuss how their pre-birth expectations are similar or different to what is happening now. The couple is not asked to negotiate changes, just discuss their perceptions. The review session is used to assist the couple to negotiate changes they wish to make.

An example of how an educator might review with a couple their discussion of the similarities and differences between pre-birth expectations and post-birth reality is illustrated by revisiting a couple, Enrico and Noi, who now have a 3-month-old baby girl, Carmen.

Educator: "How did you go looking at how you balance of time? What have you identified in your list?"

Enrico: "The baby has changed our life so much. Although we talked about sharing baby care and household chores, there's more to do than I thought. We have hardly any time together and I have no time for myself."

Educator: "Uh-huh, and what about you Noi?"

Noi: "I don't know what Enrico is saying. He leaves for work every day and has heaps of time to himself. I really wanted my mum to stay for a month after the baby was born. This is a tradition and would have really helped me out with the baby and housework. She couldn't come and I'm so disappointed. All I seem to do is look after the baby and do the housework."

Educator: "I hear that you are both feeling overwhelmed with looking after the baby, maintaining the house, and working."

Enrico: "You know I feel we should be able to look after our baby ourselves ..."
Noi: (interrupting) "but we're not coping, or at least I am not because I am here all day, every day, on my own."
Educator: "I am struck that you both are saying this is hard, harder than we thought. For you Noi there are long stretches of time when it's just you and the baby, and that can be exhausting. For Enrico, you feel its work, home and baby care, back to work. So it's hard for both of you right now?"
Noi: "Yes, and I feel I need some help."
Educator: "I would like to suggest we have you discuss this issue of how to manage feeling overwhelmed. Noi: the final step of preparation for the discussion you were asked to do was to identify a communication skill you wanted to focus upon to make the conversation productive. In talking with Enrico now, what skill would you like to focus upon?"

In the above dialog the educator starts by trying to assist the couple to clarify their use of time. The educator reflects back that both spouses are struggling, and the educator facilitates a discussion to identify different options. After discussing the communication skill Noi wished to focus upon, the educator then had Enrico identify a specific skill he wanted to use. This process prompts the couple to seek to be constructive in discussing the issue.

In the discussion the couple decided Enrico would take a week of leave, spend most of that at home to give Noi a couple of hours most days to do things other than baby care, and that he also would take a few hours here and there for things he wanted to do. The educator then explored Enrico's resistance to having Noi's mother stay over in the following interaction.

Educator: "Enrico, can you say a little more on your concerns about Noi's mother staying with you and helping out?"
Enrico: "Like I said, I sort of feel we should be able to do this as a couple, not have to rely on your Mum to help out."
Educator: "It seems kind of a failure to need help? Is that it?"
Enrico: "Yeah, I guess. It does sound a little dumb when you put it that way."
Educator: "I am thinking it must be hard for you to understand why Noi struggles during the day on her own. Maybe if you have a week at home with you doing more baby care you two will be able to talk about the challenge for Noi of lots of time at home caring for Carmen."

As it transpired Enrico got a much better idea of just how demanding caring for a young child was in the week he had at home, and agreed that Noi's mother coming to stay was a good idea. Active involvement of fathers in child care can be very helpful to developing mutual understanding of each parents' contributions, and developing an agreement on the best way forward that meets both of their needs. In exploring the balance of time it can be useful to make the point that there is no one right way to manage the early months of parenthood. The expectations people have vary by circumstances and culture. For example, some new parents have jobs that allow them parental leave, others do not, and this greatly affects the options open to the couple. Some new parents have enough money to buy in some help to assist with shopping, laundry and food preparation but many couples do not. Some couples have extended family nearby who are willing to help, others couples do not. Couples need to find the best way for them, based on shared and realistic expectations about how they will manage parenthood. By the end of this review of division of labor the couple should have negotiated what they jointly want to change (with the educator's facilitation), made concrete change plans for achieving the change(s), and set a review date for when they would review if the change was achieving its aims.

Reviewing Social Support

Another important goal of the current unit is to help partners understand the different types of support, and evaluate what sort of support they currently offer their partner. Then the couple is assisted to set goals of any changes required to provide the desired support. The educator should ask each partner to describe their answers to the form presented as Table 6.5. It is useful to highlight the sort of support each person provides for the other and the best aspect of receiving that support.

Partner support usually takes one of three forms: emotional support, problem solving support, and practical support. Emotional support is listening to your partner and simply trying to understand. Problem solving support is discussing options to solve a problem. Practical support is doing something for your partner that is helpful. A common error people make is providing the wrong sort of support, of not recognizing what sort of support their partner really wants. A common example of mismatched support is women who are seeking emotional support, but their partner provides problem solving support. A common way women describe this experience is: "he doesn't listen to me; he just keeps telling me what to do." A common way men describe this is: "I try to help, suggest things she might try, but it seems whatever I suggest is wrong."

Practice Tip
Explain the three different sorts of support and ask each person to identify what sort of support they would find most helpful for the things they are finding stressful.

The level of support the partners provide to each other, and the support each receives from others outside the couple relationship, vary considerably between couples. While availability of support is important, satisfaction with the available support is also important. Satisfaction with the level of partner support has many benefits. For example, when fathers are actively involved with infant care and household chores, and also emotionally validate the mother, the mother is more likely to report high maternal well-being, relationship satisfaction and show high parenting sensitivity.

New fathers, on the other hand, report high relationship satisfaction, and interact at high rates with their baby when they receive support from their partners in balancing male work and family roles. Thus, mutual support enhances couple relationship satisfaction, and both partners active involvement with infant care.

Self-Change Plan

The Unit 4 review sessions ends with a discussion of each partner's self-change plan. The educator should ask each person what they have identified as one area in their relationship discussed in the current unit that they would like to change. At this point in the program the partners have developed and implemented a number of self-change plans. In most couples partners at this point are able to identify specific actions, but it remains important to review the self-change plans of each partner. If the review session has prompted reconsideration of some issues, then one or both partners might want to modify their personal self-change plan. If that is the case encourage the person to choose an area that is important to them and follow the self-change plan process addressed in previous units (describe, focus, set goal, and evaluate).

Challenges in Offering This Unit

The Couple Has Not Completed the Self-Directed Learning Activities

Some couples do not complete the suggested self-directed learning activities. To reduce the chance of this occurring it can be useful to remind couples (e.g., via text, telephone call or email) of the need to complete tasks a day or two before the review session is scheduled. If the couple has not completed any activities then it is usually preferable to reschedule the review session. Before doing that the educator should go through a similar three-step reviews process as described in Chap. 4 for discussing incomplete self-change plan implementation. First, the educator checks whether the couple understood what they were asked to do in the self-directed learning component. Second, the educator explores each partner's thoughts about completing the task. Finally the educator discusses with the couple any barriers to completing the tasks, and problem solves with the couple how to overcome these barriers. The discussion might go something like the following example.

Sylvia: "Sorry but we had a really tough week and we have not got it done."

Educator: "OK, these things happen. I understand things can get hectic with a young babe. I would like to just check a couple of things. Just to be sure I was clear in explaining the self-directed exercises; can you tell me what you two thought you were meant to do before the review session tonight?"

Jurgen: "We had to work our way through the task in the handouts you gave us?"

Educator: "Right, and complete the forms in there on your views of how you are adjusting to parenthood, and talk though your answers together. So it seems you were clear on what to do. I want to ask for your honest thoughts on this, tell me what you really think about doing these tasks Sylvia."

Sylvia: "Oh, OK I guess"

Educator: "OK? Do you think doing them would be helpful?"

Sylvia: "Maybe. I sort of feel we are doing OK, and wonder if we really need to do this."

Educator: "Jurgen, Sylvia is wondering if you two are likely to get anything really useful from doing this. What are your thoughts?"

Jurgen: "Mmmh, I am not sure …"

Educator: "Is it fair to say you both feel you are managing parenthood reasonably well? (Sylvia and Jurgen both agree). OK, and in doing well you are sort of questioning do we need to be doing the exercises and reviewing things?"

Sylvia: "I guess so."

Educator: "Sound like maybe you're not sure, maybe completing the program might be helpful, maybe not?"

Jurgen: "Last night we planned to do the tasks, but we were both whacked. Elsie kept us up the night before, and I said to Sylvia 'do we really need to do this?' The TV was on, and we got a little distracted, and then I fell asleep. So it never happened."

Educator: "So you're both feeling tired, thinking about doing the tasks, wondering if you really need the program. In the end it is entirely up to you if you want to keep doing the program. Some couples doing well decide not to do all the units, and that is fine. I would like to take just a couple of minutes to chat about the pros and cons for you of continuing. Would that be OK?"

Jurgen: "Sure."

Sylvia: "Mhh hmm."

Educator: "One thing I find in working with couples who are adjusting well to parenthood is that the activities and review sessions often reinforce what people are doing right. It helps couples to feel good about what they are doing right. Also because couples find different aspects of parenthood challenging, a couple who feel all is good in one unit might find something useful in another unit to address something they are finding challenging. Like the current unit is mainly focused on sharing tasks, and the use of time and support needs. The next unit is couple intimacy. This focuses on affection and managing restarting sex. So you might want to have a go at the current unit, if you think reviewing what is going well is useful. Or, you might decide to skip this unit and go to the next one on intimacy and sexuality. Or, you might decide you do not wish to continue on. Jurgen: What are your thoughts?"

Jurgen: "Um, I feel we are doing OK but I am a little concerned about sex you know. I would like to do the next unit."

Educator: "Thank you for telling me Jurgen. Sylvia: What are your thoughts about doing the current or next unit? What do you think of the idea of moving to the next unit?"

In the example above, the educator first reviews with the couple potential barriers to completing the unit. The educator learns that the couple understood the tasks, but did not feel a particular need for the content covered. The educator then negotiates with the couple about how to proceed. It is important to be explicit in negotiating with couples when tasks are not being completed. The couple is, of course, entitled to withdraw from the program if they wish. At the same time it can be helpful to discuss with them the options, and negotiate exactly how the couple wishes to proceed.

The Couple Feels No Need To Do a Self-Change Plan

For some couples this unit is easily and quickly completed because they are satisfied with the division of labor in their relationship, happy with the support they provide each other and receive from others, and feel their balance of time use is appropriate. For such couples there might be little or no change either partner desires. In our experience some educators feel unsure what to do when the couple is highly satisfied with their current adjustment to parenthood. It is entirely legitimate for couples to determine their current way of managing parenthood is working for them, and the educator should accept this view.

At the same time the educator can play an important role in reinforcing the positive way each partner is adapting to parenthood. This is best done by encouraging the partners to be specific in describing what they themselves have done to make the transition to parenthood work well, and to have them comment on what their partner is doing that makes things go smoothly. It is also worth exploring with the couple what they can do to maintain the positive coping strategies they are using. An example of a productive review session with such a couple is illustrated below.

Educator:	"It seems then that both of you are pretty happy with how you have adapted to parenthood? Is that right?"
Kevin:	"Yeah, I think so. We both get tired at times, being woken in the night can be tough, but we are managing I think."
Aya:	"I do get tired some days, especially if Aynn has been not slept much during the day. But Kevin takes over Aynn's care when he gets home and gives me a chance to have a break and a nap."
Educator:	"So Kevin providing that back up really helps?"
Aya:	"Oh, yeah. And on weekends too, he will give me a couple of hours to have lunch with a friend. Or when we all go to the shops he is on Aynn care duty so I can do things."
Educator (laughing):	"Sounds like you have him well trained."
Aya:	"He is good."
Educator:	"So Kevin, it seems Aya finds the child care you do really makes a big difference to her."
Kevin:	"Aya has had back problems, so I try to do as much of the Aynn lifting as I can – you know bathing her at night, and doing the nappy changes when I am not at work."

Educator: "Fantastic, Kevin's contribution to the parenting team seems to be working well for you both. Kevin: Aya says she feels things are going pretty well. What do think Aya does to make it work?"

Kevin: "She reminds me to make this whole time fun. Like yesterday it was warm. When I came in after work Aya had Aynn's gear all loaded up in the pusher and we went down to the park with snacks and drinks. Aynn loves the park; she looks around at the big kids running around."

Educator; "So Aya put in the preparation so you could have family time in the park, and sounds like you really appreciated that."

Kevin: "Yeah, absolutely."

Introducing Unit 5 Caring and Sexuality

The next unit in Couple CARE for Parents is on intimacy and sexuality. In ending the current session it is important to set a date for the next review session, and discuss with the couple the key tasks for the next unit. This unit is usually delivered in flexible delivery mode. Hence, the materials need to be provided to the couple at least a week ahead of the scheduled review session.

An example introduction to the caring activities is provided below for educators who wish to provide a rationale for the importance of reviewing caring.

"*When couples first get together they tend to do lots of caring things for each other. But, after a while these acts of caring can drop off. Sometimes caring between partners dramatically decreases when they become parents. This can happen for any number of reasons such as feeling too tired, being too busy, feeling disconnected from each other, the woman's changing body size, shape and function (e.g., breastfeeding), or because the baby asks for so much caring that partner's feel they can't give anymore. To keep love alive all couples need to show caring on a regular basis. Couples who don't leave time for acts of caring and affection often find that the spark goes out of their relationship. In contrast, couples who show high levels of caring in their relationship, even when managing the challenges of parenting young children, report higher relationship satisfaction. Unit 5 will explore how parenthood has changed caring in your relationship and if there are any changes you wish to make to the amount or type of caring you show each other.*"

An example introduction to the sexuality activities is also provided below and can be shared with the couple when preparing the couple for completing the unit activities.

"*This unit also includes activities focused on your sexual relationship. Some of the activities go into detail. For example, you will see there are individual activities examining your sexual self-talk, your desired frequency of sex, and your sexual likes and dislikes. I am happy to discuss any aspect of your sexual relationship. However your privacy will be respected at all times. Please feel free to share as much or as little about aspects of your sex life. If you do not want to discuss your answers to an activity which I ask you about, please let me know and we shall move on to the next activity.*"

The educator may like to share some or all of the following guidelines about how the couple can negotiate completing the activities at home, and how the phone review session will review the sexuality activities:

1. *Many people feel a bit uncomfortable when talking about sex. If you find such discussion difficult, it can be useful to tell this to your partner.*
2. *Only disclose as much in your writing and speaking as you feel comfortable with.*
3. *Respect your partner's privacy. Please do not read what he or she has written or push him or her to speak about things he or she is uncomfortable with.*
4. *There might be topics you want to discuss with your partner, but not with me as your educator. That is OK.*

The educator can then ask the couple if they have any questions or concerns about the next unit.

Chapter 7
Caring and Sexuality

Chapter Highlights

- Prompt self-reflection and partner feedback on expressions of caring.
- Address varying degrees of comfort partners have in discussing sexual matters.
- Challenge unhelpful self-talk about sexuality.
- Develop shared realistic beliefs about sex after childbirth and the couple's capacity to communicate about sexual issues.
- Assist couples to enjoy sexual intimacy.

This chapter describes common difficulties couples may experience in having time for each other, for expressing caring, and for re-establishing a healthy sex life after the birth of their child. In this unit on caring and sexuality, the educator assists the couple to review and enhance their expression of caring toward each other. Couples discuss the effects of pregnancy, childbirth, and parenting on their sex life; review their current sexual practices, and how they communicate about sexuality. The aim of the unit is to help partners develop shared realistic expectations about caring and sex in the early months after childbirth, and to identify and implement self-change to enhance intimacy in their relationship.

The current unit follows the same general structure as previous units. It begins with a review of the previous unit's self-change plan on sharing infant care, introduces the new content on couple caring and sexuality, and culminates in the development of a self-change plan in the areas covered in the unit. The content of the unit is summarized in Table 7.1.

Like the previous unit, this unit is also delivered in a flexible-delivery format, where couples independently complete the unit activities and steps 1–3 of the self-change

Electronic Supplementary Material: The online version of this chapter (doi:10.1007/978-1-4939-1613-9_7) contains supplementary material, which is available to authorized users.

W.K. Halford et al., *Clinical Guide to Helping New Parents*,
Springer Series on Couples and Health, DOI 10.1007/978-1-4939-1613-9_7

Table 7.1 Content and activities for caring and sexuality

Topic and aim	Tasks	Example activity
Self-Change Review	Review each partners' self-change plan	Review the success of Unit 4 self-change plan step 4 (evaluation)
Caring Behaviors	Introduce importance of caring behaviors Outline some of the changes in caring behavior that can occur with parenthood Partner feedback on showing caring Enhance or maintain high levels of caring	Identifying impact of parenthood on levels and type of caring List caring behaviors partner does Identify caring behavior to do over next week
Prepare couples to discuss sexuality	Introduce guidelines for exploring couple sexuality	
Sexuality and new parenthood	Review common sex self-talk readings If negative sex self-talk exists review with the partner how he/she went about changing the negative sex self-talk to positive sex self-talk	Reading common sex self-talk Challenging negative or unhelpful sex self-talk
Couple discussion of sexuality	Review of couples current sexual frequency, likes and dislikes, and be available to discuss discrepancy or concerns. Couple communication about sex	Sexual frequency checklist Sexual likes and dislikes checklist Sexual strengths and challenges
Self-change plan	To review the couples steps 1–3 self-change plan for Unit 6	

plan at home, and then review the unit with the educator in a scheduled telephone or video-conference discussion. Couples will therefore need to have access to the unit activity sheets and these can be either sent to the couple, or left with the couple at the end of the Unit 3 (Chap. 5) home visit with instructions on what to complete before each scheduled phone call with the educator. An example introduction to the caring activities is provided below for educators who wish to provide a rationale for the importance of reviewing caring.

"*When couples first get together they tend to do lots of caring things for each other. But, after a while these acts of caring can drop off. Sometimes caring between partners dramatically decreases when they become parents. This can happen for any number of reasons such as feeling too tired, being too busy, feeling disconnected from each other, the woman's changing body size, shape and function (e.g., breastfeeding), or because the baby asks for so much caring that partner's feel they can't give anymore. To keep love alive all couples need to show caring on a regular basis. Couples who don't leave time for acts of caring and affection often find that the spark goes out of their relationship. In contrast, couples who show high levels of caring in their relationship, even when managing the challenges of parenting young children, report higher relationship satisfaction.*"

An example introduction to the sexuality activities is also provided below and can be shared with the couple when preparing the couple for completing the unit activities.

"This unit includes activities focused on your sexual relationship. Some of the activities go into detail. For example, you will see there are individual activities examining your sexual self-talk, your desired frequency of sex, and your sexual likes and dislikes. I am happy to discuss any aspect of your sexual relationship. However your privacy will be respected at all times. Please feel free to share as much or as little about aspects of your sex life as you choose. If you do not want to discuss your answers to an activity which I ask you about, please let me know and we shall move on to the next activity."

The educator may like to share some or all of the following guidelines about how the couple can negotiate completing the activities at home, and how the phone review session will review the sexuality activities:

1. *Many people feel a bit uncomfortable when talking about sex. If you find such discussion difficult, it can be useful to tell this to your partner.*
2. *Only disclose as much in your writing and speaking as you feel comfortable with.*
3. *Respect your partner's privacy. Please do not read what he or she has written or push him or her to speak about things he or she is uncomfortable with.*
4. *There might be topics you want to discuss with your partner, but not with me as your educator. That is OK.*

Caring

High levels of expression of caring promote a sense of intimacy between partners, and this is associated with enhanced couple relationship satisfaction. Moreover, high rates of expression of caring buffer the damaging effects of negative couple communication, and promotes more father involvement in parenting. Although being a parent of a baby is very time-consuming, many couples report that by about 3 months after the birth, the demands of infant care moderate somewhat. Often (although not in all families) the baby is waking less at night, which allows an improvement in the parents' sleep. Parents have developed more confidence, and competence, in managing the challenges of infant care. Partners often feel they have the time and energy to refocus some attention to their couple relationship.

Enhancing caring can be challenging, but at the same time is particularly important especially for certain couples who have experienced the following:

- parenthood has reduced the frequency of caring;
- caring behaviors have reduced over time for other reasons;
- partners value different type of caring behavior from that which their partner is currently providing;
- caring behaviors frequency is highly unequal (one partner doing a lot more acts of caring than the other).

An observation you might like to share with couples is that most new mothers find a particularly strong benefit from high levels of caring by their partner in the early months of parenthood. Often the new mother is caring for the baby full-time and finds it hard to also get household chores completed, or to get enough sleep, let alone have much time for herself. It is very helpful when fathers increase their contribution to household chores, express affection, and show caring toward their partner (e.g., they smile at their partner, kiss their partner, touch them affectionately, and let their partner sleep in). At the same time, the heavy demands on new mothers often mean her caring toward her partner diminishes. This unequal level of caring behaviors—brought on in association with parenthood—can cause strain and resentment in some fathers. It is important for mothers to notice and express appreciation for the caring shown by the father. Moreover, it is important that mothers try to increase their caring expressed toward their partner, and not let an unbalanced expression of caring continue in the long-term.

Clinical Connection
What makes it hard to show caring in your relationship? How could you use your experiences to helpfully illustrate the points below?

Some useful points educators can make about successful caring include the following:

1. There are different ways to show caring.
2. Different people value receiving different caring behaviors.
3. It can be a challenge to identify and do the caring behaviors that your partner most values.
4. Doing new and different caring behaviors is important to keep caring meaningful for partners. (Bringing home chocolates on a Friday night is nice, but its meaning is diminished if it becomes a predictable habit.)
5. We need to show caring even when things are not going well in the relationship.

When reviewing the activities in this unit it can be helpful to start with a question such as: "*What positive effects has parenthood had on the amount and type of caring you have shown your partner in the last few weeks?*" or "*What negative effects has parenthood had on the amount and type of caring you have shown your partner in the last few weeks?*"

Educators can reflect and summarize the couple's current experience of caring, and the influences on expressions of caring. It can be useful to then ask each partner to turn to the *Caring Behaviors Checklist* shown in Table 7.2 and share the top three caring behaviors they most like from their partner. It can also be helpful to ask what effect feeling cared for has on each partner and to then summarize the key points the couple have made about caring for each other.

Table 7.2 Caring behaviors checklist

Caring things my partner does (or has done) for me	Tick the behaviors I like most
1	
2	
3	
4	
5	
6	
7	
8	
9	
10	

Practice Tip
Psychological research points to two aspects of caring that are crucial in enhancing couple relationships. First, novelty in expressing caring enhances passion. This means that couples who are creative, and find new ways to express caring toward each other, experience more sustained passion in their relationship. Second, when each partner is seen by the other to be making an effort to express caring, it creates a virtuous cycle. That is, if one partner does something caring (without being asked) that prompts the other partner to also do something caring. That sets up a positive cycle of each person expressing caring for the other.

Sexual Intimacy

The sexuality section of this unit includes discussion about sex after childbirth, and several individual activities examining each partner's sexual self-talk, their desired frequency of sex, sexual likes and dislikes, and communication about sexuality. Sexual likes and dislikes can change across the transition to parenthood, so it is timely to have partners review what each prefers. The key goals during the discussions on sexuality are to foster shared, realistic beliefs about sex after childbirth; encourage positive and helpful sexual self-talk; enhance the couple's capacity to communicate effectively about sexual issues; and assist them to further enhance their enjoyment of their sexual relationship.

When running Couple CARE for Parents, the gender of the educator can influence how comfortable participants are in discussing their sexual concerns. Often we have had female educators running the program and find the female partners are typically the first to self-disclose about sexual concerns and thoughts. In particular, women often reported concerns about discrepancy in desire and frequency of sex, and pain during sex to female educators. On occasions when male educators have facilitated Couple CARE for Parents, women seemed less likely to open up about their sexual concerns. Male educators can enhance women's comfort disclosing by noting that while they are not female, and cannot experience birth personally and its associated changes they have listened to lots of women's stories and are comfortable listening and supporting women, and men in discussing sexuality after childbirth.

Interestingly male participants often seem reluctant, at least initially, to volunteer comments about their sexual concerns to either male or female educators. Yet research shows men often do have concerns. Educators can assist men to self-disclose by noting how many men are initially slow to talk about such issues. When inviting couples to ask questions about sex after childbirth, educators can model being open about sex. In this chapter we provide several examples of how educators can introduce a review of an activity, or provide psycho-education, using clear open language about sexuality.

Practice Tip
Throughout these activities on sexuality it is important for the educator to be sensitive to disclosures about sexuality. In this unit participants may use vague statements, jokes, or colloquialisms rather than clear descriptions of behaviors. We have found it useful for educators to use some of the same terms as the couple, but also to use explicit sexual language to encourage the partners to be specific and open up about the issues.

Sexuality in the Perinatal Period

Most couples' sexual relationship is vulnerable to deterioration across pregnancy and in the first year after the birth of their child. Almost all couples decrease the frequency of sex during the third trimester of pregnancy, and many couples stop all sexual activity. Many things contribute to this decline in sexual activity including increasing fatigue in the woman as pregnancy progresses, physical discomfort in particular sexual positions, and feelings of decreased sexual attractiveness (for the woman) and attraction (for the man) as the woman's body changes. It can be useful to mention that these changes are common in most couples' sex life during pregnancy. Most couples resume sexual activity at some point between 4 weeks and 10 weeks after the birth, and often begin with oral sex or masturbation before resuming intercourse (Hipp et al., 2012). Typically couples' frequency and enjoyment of sexual activity increases across the first year after the birth of their child. This information could be shared with a comment such as the following:

"On average, couples resume sexual intercourse 6 to 10 weeks after birth, but there is no one right time to start. Some women find their vagina is tender or dry, or that the perineum (the skin between the vagina and the anus) is tender. Some men

worry that inserting their penis in their partner's vagina might cause her pain. Many couples use masturbation or oral sex initially, and return to intercourse a bit later, finding that with time they can resume a satisfying sexual relationship."

However, about 25–30 % of couples report significant, ongoing sexual dissatisfaction a year after the birth of the first child (Abdool, Thanker, & Sultan, 2009).

Practice Tip
There are two strong predictors of women's sexual enjoyment in the year after childbirth. The first is sexual difficulties that existed before pregnancy. Couples who had experienced such difficulties are likely to benefit from a referral for sexual therapy. Timing of such a referral is important. Soon after birth couples often feel overwhelmed by the demands of parenting, and sex might seem to be a low priority. The educator needs to be sensitive as to when the couple might be receptive to exploring how to address sexual concerns. The second predictor is the woman's beliefs about whether her partner still finds her attractive. It can help women to know that this is a common concern. For men it can also be helpful knowing that it is a common concern, and that being romantic and caring but not sexually pushy is a helpful approach in rebuilding the woman's confidence in her sexuality.

Some brief advice around relationships and sexuality in the perinatal period can assist couples to negotiate this challenging period in their sex life. We find a couple of introductory points worth making about sex in new parents couples are as follows.

"*There is a common misunderstanding that often develops between partners around sex soon after the birth. Often couples are having sex less often, if at all, in the last month or two before the birth and in the first month or two after birth. In these times many women are looking for emotional closeness with their partner. Many women wonder if their partner still loves them and is attracted to them when their body has changed. Women often seek reassurance and closeness through cuddles and kisses. At the same time the woman might not be feeling sexy or wanting intercourse. In the context of the couple not having sex much, if the woman is affectionate the man often interprets this as the woman wanting sex. If she declines sex, he can feel hurt and confused. For men sex is often the way they feel reassured they are loved and desired.*

If the couple understand that affection seeking without sexual desire often occurs that understanding can help to prevent it becoming a problem. The man might recognize and accept his partner's needs for reassurance and affection without pressure to engage in sex. The woman might recognize and accept the man's desire for sex as part of his need for closeness and reassurance, and she can be clear when she is ready to initiate sexual activity."

Couples who are concerned about pain when initiating sexual intercourse may benefit from discussing their concerns. It is often useful to talk about things they could try to optimize their mutual enjoyment when recommencing sexual activity. The educator could say something like,

"Some discomfort for the woman during intercourse tends to occur after birth. What have you tried to reduce the pain? What else could you do to lessen any possible pain?"

If the couple asks for other suggestions the educator could offer some of the following tips:

- Experimenting with stimulation with hands or mouth is an option.
- Sex often can be made more comfortable by trying different positions for intercourse such as the man behind the woman with them lying on their side.
- Some women find their vagina lubricates less (gets less wet) after the birth, and that can make intercourse uncomfortable, particularly when the penis is entering the vagina. The use of KY gel, or other water soluble lubricant, can increase comfort. (Avoid using oils as these can clog the pores of the skin and increase the chance of infection.)
- If the woman has severe, deep seated or persistent pain then recommend the women has a check-up with her doctor.

Beliefs About Sex

The first activity covering sexuality after childbirth that the educator will review with couples is handout 7.4 covering common beliefs couples have about sexuality, and specifically sexuality as a new parent. Many of these beliefs are worth exploring and some need to be gently challenged. Couples will have been given the handout of common beliefs about sex after childbirth (see Table 7.3) at the end of the previous unit/or as a mail-out. During the phone review the educator can ask partners to comment on any statements the couple identified with a lot, a little or not at all. Introducing the review of this particular activity sensitively can enhance the likelihood that partners volunteer that they have these beliefs.

Introducing the review of sexual thoughts activity could go something like this: *"All of us have ideas about how sex should or should not be, and what our partner does and does not desire. The handout called 'Common beliefs about sex' covered some of the ideas we have come across among couples who have recently had a baby. All of these beliefs are normal reactions to post-baby experiences of intimacy. When you read through them which ones stood out for you as things you have caught yourself doing or thinking recently or sometime in the past? Did you mark any of them? Are there any you would like to talk about?"*

The information sheet provided in Table 7.4 is relevant to some of the common negative beliefs about sex. Educators might use this handout to review evidence-based information about sex after childbirth with the couple.

Clinical Connection

How comfortable are you in the role of an educator talking explicitly with a couple about sex? What words will/do you use in your role as educator in talking about penises, vaginas, intercourse, oral sex, and masturbation?

Table 7.3 Common thoughts about sex after childbirth

Common thoughts	Ever had this thought?	
Men and women		
We should be having sex by now!	Yes	No
We will never find time for sex because the baby is always there	Yes	No
Women		
My body looks terrible! I can't even think about having sex until I start to look sexier	Yes	No
The pain is bad—I never want to have sex again	Yes	No
I am never ever having another child!! (the birth was too traumatic)	Yes	No
Does he find me attractive now?	Yes	No
Men		
Is it wrong for me to want sex? How long should I wait?	Yes	No
Is even asking about sex a bad idea?		
"All she ever does is breastfeed and care for the baby – It's like I've lost my wife."	Yes	No
"Does she find me attractive now?"	Yes	No
Other thoughts you have had? "……………………………………………………………………"		
"……………………………………………………………………"		

Table 7.4 Information about common thoughts on sex after childbirth

"We should be having sex by now."
Couples vary a lot in how soon they resume having sexual intercourse after the birth of their baby. There is no correct time, though couples are often told that sex can be resumed anywhere between 6 and 9 weeks after birth. Interactions about resuming sex can sometimes be a source of strain between partners. Often, but not always, the man is the first to initiate after the birth. If the woman does not feel ready or interested, she will often reject the advance. If repeated, this can set up an unfortunate pattern of the man initiating and the woman rejecting. This pattern can make the woman feel pressured to have sex and resentful of that pressure, while the man feels rejected and unloved Talking about sex, when not in bed, can help. Making sure you have some quality time as a couple also helps. Expressing caring toward each other can help develop the feelings that make sex more appealing. It is important to remember it takes time for the woman's body to heal, for sexual desire to return (in either partner), and that this intense newborn phase will pass. Both of partners are making a lot of changes, and it is important to be gentle with each other
"My body looks terrible!"
A woman's body changes enormously with pregnancy and childbirth. Some women feel acutely aware of their body shape and need reassurance from their partner that they are still attractive. For both partners leading a healthy lifestyle can help them feel physically better and more interested in sex. Some gentle exercise 3–4 times per week, watching their diet, not smoking, and limiting drinking of alcohol to not more than two drinks per day for men or women (except during breastfeeding when no alcohol is the safest), will help a couple get (or stay) in shape. A healthy lifestyle will help each partner feel better about their appearance, and to manage the demands of being a parent

(continued)

Table 7.4 (continued)

"Sex is uncomfortable"
Many women experience some physical trauma during childbirth. Healing needs to occur before intercourse is comfortable. Even if the couple leave 6–8 weeks after the birth for healing to occur, about half of all women report some discomfort in the first few attempts to have intercourse after birth. Sex is rarely as good soon after birth as it was before the pregnancy or birth. About 25 % of women do not experience orgasm for up to 6 months post-partum. If couples are informed about these physical changes, accept this, take it slowly, and talk together, most couples report a gradual improvement in their sex life
"The baby is always there"
It can be difficult for both partners to juggle caring for their baby, keeping the household running, and doing their job. Women, in particular, often feel that their primary responsibility is baby care, and many women report they hardly even think about sex. For the man this can be experienced as a loss of intimacy, and as a rejection by their partner
"She/He/We are avoiding sex"
It is important to recognize that the first 6 months or so after the birth of a child is a time of change. A bit of struggling at this time to find time or interest in sex is common, and does not mean you have fallen out of love, or anything is terribly wrong. Using ideas like good communication, showing caring, providing mutual support, and planning shared activities can help to keep a positive relationship focus
This is but one point in our life together
Some people worry that their sex life is forever changed by parenthood. Recognizing that sexual activity tends to vary across along life together, and that the early months of parenthood pass quickly can be useful

Table 7.5 Sex self-talk example monitoring form

1. Situation	2. My self-talk about sex	3. Positive self-talk to replace negative self-talk
Man example: I cuddled up to Liz in bed and started to fondle her. She pushed me away and went quiet	God, not again. What is the problem? OK she's tired, but she's always tired. I'm tired, but I still have feelings	OK, she probably is tired. Neither of us got much sleep last night. I know it's hard for many women to feel sexy when they're breast feeding. Liz and I should talk about this, tomorrow, when we're less tired
Woman example: Mike cuddled up to me and started to fondle me. I pushed him away and ignored him	What is the problem? Doesn't he know I am exhausted, and my boobs feel bloated? How can he think about sex?	Neither of us got much sleep last night. We are not having sex, and Mike wants to feel close (and he is horny, which at least shows he fancies me). Mike and I should talk about this, tomorrow, when we're less tired

The next exercise requires couples to spend a week recording their own thoughts about sex and intimacy using the handout 7.6 entitled *My Sexual Self-Talk.* The handout 7.5 is an example of how this form could be filled out.

The activity is intended to provide partners with the opportunity to record and reflect on their personal sexual self-talk. The handouts have the same layout as those provided in Chap. 5 (Unit 3 section on identifying and challenging negative

Table 7.6 Sex self-talk monitoring form
On your own, at the end of each day for the next week record any sex self-talk you had that day. In column 1 write the situation in which the self-talk occurred. Write your self-talk in column. Circle any sex self-talk that is negative or unhelpful. In column 3 try to write down more positive and helpful self-talk. You might like to talk about what you write with your partner, and ask them what positive self-talk you could use

1. Situation	2. My self-talk about sex	3. Positive self-talk to replace negative self-talk

self-talk). The aim of the activity is to identify if negative or unhelpful self-talk is occurring for either partner on anything related to sexual intimacy. After completing the recording sheet independently the couple is asked to sit and share some of their self-talk with their partner before the phone call with the educator. During the phone review session educators could open this discussion with a prompt such as: "*When you recorded your own self-talk about sex over the last week/fortnight what did you learn? Did you have negative, unhelpful self-talk for which you generated alternative helpful and positive self-talk*?" If either partner has identified negative and unhelpful self-talk is can be helpful to check in with the other partner if they were aware of the negative and unhelpful self-talk before doing this activity and how they might support their partner to develop more positive helpful self-talk around this issue.

Practice Tip
If you run Couple Care for Parents in a group setting, it can be useful to invite people to write down questions they have about sex after childbirth. The educator can then collect these pieces of paper and give advice to the whole group on each question without requiring participants to state their questions or concerns out loud.

Sexual Frequency

The next two activities look at what is currently happening in the couples' sex life with the aim of helping partners identify what they want from their sexual relationship. Before reviewing these activities with the couple remind them that they can decline to discuss anything they wish to keep private, but that you are happy to go into details if they find that helpful. Table 7.7 is a handout that lists a series of questions about the frequency of sex across four time periods in the couple's

Table 7.7 Sexual frequency during our relationship
Do this exercise on your own, then discuss with your partner

1. When we first started living together we had sex:	Place a tick for your answer
(a) More than four times per week	
(b) 3–4 times per week	
(c) 1–2 times a week	
(d) 1–2 times a fortnight	
(e) once per month or less	
2. In the 6 months before pregnancy we had sex:	
(a) More than four times per week	
(b) 3–4 times per week	
(c) 1–2 times a week	
(d) 1–2 times a fortnight	
(e) Once per month or less	
3. In the last three months of pregnancy we had sex:	
(a) More than four times per week	
(b) 3–4 times per week	
(c) 1–2 times a week	
(d) 1–2 times a fortnight	
(e) Once a month or less	
4. How often would you like to have sex now?	
(a) More than four times per week	
(b) 3–4 times per week	
(c) 1–2 times a week	
(d) 1–2 times a fortnight	
(e) Once a month or less	

5. Since having your baby have you resumed sex? Yes/No?
If **no**: What are your thoughts about resuming sex?
………………………………………………………………………………………
………………………………………………………………………………………
If **yes**: Take a few notes here about how sex is going
………………………………………………………………………………………
………………………………………………………………………………………

relationship: in the early stages of their relationship, just before the pregnancy, during pregnancy, and what they want now after the birth.

Some couples wonder what frequency of sex is normal. Educators might like to provide some education about the frequency of sex typically reported by studies on couples' sex lives. For example, the educator might say: "*Some couples wonder about what is normal in terms of the frequency of having sex, especially after having a baby. Some may ask themselves when will sex get back to the frequency it was before the baby. Research shows that most couples have sex frequently early on in their relationship. In national surveys couples in their 20's tend to have sex anything from once per week to daily, with the average being 2–3 times per week. During pregnancy frequency usually declines, and some couples won't have sex in the last 1–2 months of pregnancy. Doctors typically advise couples to wait at least six weeks after the birth before resuming sexual intercourse, and most couples resume sex between 6–10 weeks after birth. Almost all women, and some men, report lower sexual desire for a time after the birth of their child. Pregnancy, birth and breastfeeding each affect a woman's body, changing her hormone levels, and the shape of her body and breasts. If the woman is breastfeeding she will produce less of the hormone which provides lubrication during intercourse. Both men and women sometimes view breastfeeding mothers' breasts differently, and this can also affect sexual desire.*

By 6 months after the birth most couples have successfully resumed sex. Most couples report that intimacy has gradually become mutually enjoyable again. However, up to one-quarter of couples experience ongoing difficulty with sex, with some women still reporting pain during sex and/or low desire for sex. There is therefore a lot of variability".

The educator can invite the partners to discuss frequency of sex in their life and be available to respond to concerns or questions. However, if the couple decline to discuss their checklist with the educator, that is fine too. If a couple is interested in discussing this activity then the educator might ask: "*How has the frequency of sex changed across time, especially from when you met to now – as new parents?*" If the couple have not yet resumed sex you may like to ask: "*When would each of you like to resume sex?*" If the couple has resumed sex ask them: "*How is sex going?*"

It might help couples to know that many couples report discrepancy in desire for sex after childbirth, with men typically wanting sex more frequently than women. For most new parents infrequent sex up to 6 months post birth is common and not reflective of a pervasive problem. However, if the couple report that they had different desire for frequency of sex prior to pregnancy, and that this discrepancy is continuing, then it might be useful to refer the couple to their doctor. Some common medical conditions (e.g., chronic pain, depression) or medications (e.g., antihypertensive or antidepressant medication) can contribute to low sexual desire.

Sexual Likes and Dislikes

The aim of this activity is for partners to review with each other the range of sensual and sexual behaviors they enjoy, and identify any changes they might like to make in their sex life. Sometimes partners' preferences change as they become parents. For example, women might enjoy their nipples being caressed before pregnancy, but have different feelings when breastfeeding. Couples need to have received and completed handout 7.8 before the telephone or video-conference review with the educator. Handout 7.8 lists a wide variety of sexual behaviors. Partners are asked to individually mark down how they feel about each behavior, and then have a conversation about their answers with their partner.

A few words to introduce the review of this activity might go as follows. "*Some couples often talk openly about sex; other couples tend to communicate by nudges,*

Table 7.8 Clarifying sexual likes and dislikes
After having a baby it is very likely that a woman's sexual preferences (and sometimes the man's) will have changed. Tick one of the boxes for each of the following activities which best describes how much you like the activity. (Remember: you can choose not to speak about these details with your educator.)

Activity	Love the way we do it now	It's pretty good as it is	It's OK but we could make it better	Haven't done this but would like to try it	Don't want to do this
Initiating sex with my partner					
Having my partner initiate sex					
Kissing each other for more than 1 min					
Telling my partner my fantasies					
Having my partner tell me his/her fantasies					
Giving my partner a non-genital massage					
Receiving a non-genital massage					
Caressing my partner's nipples/other non-genital area he/she finds stimulating with my hands or lips					
Having my partner caress my nipples/other non-genital area with her/his hands or lips					
Caressing my partner's genitals with my hands					
Having my partner caress my genitals with his/her hands					
Giving my partner oral sex					
Receiving oral sex from my partner					
Giving and receiving oral sex simultaneously with my partner					
Watching my partner masturbate					
Having my partner watch me masturbate					
Mutual masturbation					
Having intercourse in the following positions (fill in) 1. 2. 3. 4.					
Other:					
Other:					

My communication strengths when discussing sexual intimacy with my partner are: …..
……………………………………………………………………………………………..
My challenges when communication about sexual intimacy with my partner: …………..
…………………………………………………………………………………………………

winks and hints. If you want we can talk about your sexual like and dislikes that you each noted when doing this activity. But if you want to keep those likes and dislikes private to the two of you, that is fine as well. Would you like to share some of your responses? (Leave time for the couple to start discussing likes/dislikes)." The educator should summarize what the partner(s) have said. If partners have discrepancies in their likes and dislikes the educator could ask them how they have managed this so far, how willing a partner is to experiment with new things the other partner might want to try, and what would make it safe or comfortable for the partner. If the couple or a partner has concerns or questions it may be helpful to assist the couple to problem solve what they could do, e.g., what options do they think they have, what might others do in this circumstance?

Even if the couple do not want to discuss the sexual likes and dislikes activity it is important for the educator to explore the couples communication about sex. This could be introduced with the following: "*One thing that I would like to cover in this review is how you communicate as a couple about sexuality. When you did the sexual likes and dislikes activity what were some good things about how you talked to each other about sex? What were some challenges in talking together about sex? After doing this activity are there things about sex that you have concerns or questions about?*"

Practice Tip

While some couples are uncomfortable divulging the details of their sexual likes and dislikes to their educator, most couples are comfortable discussing how they communicate about sex. Asking partners to share their communication strengths and areas to work on when they discuss sexual intimacy is a useful way for educators to be available for couples to debrief about this activity without pressuring couples to discuss anything they wish to keep private.

The following dialog illustrates how an educator can facilitate a review with a couple who completed the sexual communication exercise.

Educator: "*When you did the sexual likes and dislikes activity what were some good things you listed about how you talk to each other about sex?*"

Melanie: "*We did this one by ticking the boxes and then swapping books – some of it was pretty explicit and I didn't feel up to saying all of the things by name.*"

Quentin: "*I liked this activity – it helped me because I thought Mel would have written 'no – don't want to do this' on many of the activities we've not done before, but she didn't. It surprised me!*"

Educator: "*Sounds like doing the activity as a paper and pencil activity meant you could be a bit more honest than you would usually have been Melanie, and this was helpful to Quentin. It's common for couples to not describe specifics when talking about sexual preferences. Is this a challenge for you?*"

Melanie: *"Yes, it is for me. We don't talk about what we like or don't like. I usually follow Quentin's lead, and he usually gets it right".*

Educator: *"So a challenge for you, Melanie, is communicating verbally – using some of the speaker skills we covered earlier in Couple CARE for Parents. What about for you Quentin, did you note any challenges in communicating about sex?*

Quentin: *"Yes, I think that a challenge for me in knowing what the other wants – I am not always sure if Melanie is into it, if she likes what I am doing. Which is why this exercise was helpful – I got to know her a bit better. I think a challenge for me is not to jump to conclusions – make assumptions."*

Educator: *"What you are saying Quentin is that sometimes when we don't discuss sexual preferences we can end up misunderstanding our partner's thoughts, feelings or wishes. Is that right?"*

Quentin: *"Yeh... like I have noticed Mel not being that into it these last few weeks and I am not sure why, if it is something I am doing wrong – I'm not sure if she is distracted or it's not feeling good... The sexual like and dislikes form kind of tells me nothing is wrong, but I am not sure."*

Educator: *"It sounds like you have some questions – if there is something wrong? I wonder how you could check that out with Melanie?"*

Quentin: *"I could ask her, but we are not the couple to usually do that."*

Educator: *"Melanie, are there any ways that you would find it easier to communicate about sex with Quentin? Especially if he has worries?"*

Melanie: *"I am thinking that writing it down and giving me some time to answer might work...so I am not on the spot you know. Like when we did the exercise in the book, that was ok. I definitely don't want Quentin to think there is something wrong with what he is doing. I think I have been feeling like it's hard to stay in the mood...I get distracted by the baby stirring... and sometimes I am too sleepy..."*

The dialog shows how the educator's paraphrasing and questions leads to the couple—especially the male partner—to be more comfortable talking through their concerns about sex, and helps them clarify misunderstandings which may have caused difficulty in the future. The educator might next begin to explore what each partner could do to help them have fewer misunderstanding and more open communication in the future.

The last activity of Unit 5 is development of a self-change plan, focused on couple caring, intimacy and sex, or communication about sexual intimacy. The handouts from this unit can be good resources to help partners choose their self-change goal. As usual educators should ask each partner to share their self-change plan with the educator—with the preface that the partner can choose to keep the details of a sexual self-change plan private if they prefer not to share it with the educator. Even if couples do not want to disclose exactly what they are working on in a self-change plan focused on sexuality, the educator can still assist them to have a good plan. The educator can ask the following. "*Without telling me explicitly what you are working on, do you feel the self-change you have in mind is important? By important I mean that doing this would help your relationship? Is your action plan specific? (Could we record you doing this and agree it has been done?). How sure are you that you will do this action in the next week from 0 – no chance I will do this to 10 – absolutely certain I will do this?"*

Practice Tip
With the next unit being the last unit of Couple CARE for Parents, and therefore the last opportunity the educator will have to assist couples review their self-change plans it can be useful for the educator to check with partners if there was an area they would like to work on but have not yet written a self-change plan for. If so, the educator could invite the partner(s) to write an additional self-change plan at this point to be reviewed next session.

Managing Common Challenges in Running This Unit

A Partner/Couple Cannot Think of Any Caring Behaviors They Could Do for Their Partner

In the event that one or both partners find it difficult to identify caring behaviors they can do, the list of possible caring behaviors included as Table 7.9 is useful. Even when partners are happy with the frequency and types of caring behaviors currently displayed in their relationship we encourage couples to identify one or two new caring behaviors they could do for their partner in the next week. Making a little extra effort to do new behaviors can create really positive feelings between partners.

A Partner/Couple Has Not Shown Caring Toward the Other Due to Negative Feelings Toward Each Other/Is Waiting for Their Partner to Show Caring First

We find it is useful to talk to this point. The educator could say something like the following. "*A key idea here is to do your part. That is, regardless of what your partner might or might not do, you can show caring. We find that when one person shows caring it often elicits caring from the other person. We call this a virtuous cycle, where one person's positivity encourages the other, and creates a self-perpetuating system.*"

It is striking that most people thank friends, extended family, even strangers for their acts of caring. Yet sometimes we fail to express such warmth or gratitude toward our partner. For example, if you dropped something at a bus stop and a stranger picked it up most of us would thank the person. Similarly, if you went to a friend's house for dinner it would be usual to thank them for preparing the meal. Yet we often take what our partners does for us, like picking up something for us, or preparing a meal, for granted and fail to say thank you. It can be useful to remind couples of the need to show appreciation of caring behaviors by their partner.

Table 7.9 Ideas for caring behaviors

Getting a household repair done	Balancing the chequebook
Preparing an entire meal	Paying a bill
Helping with the dinner	Doing some needed gardening
Taking care of the car	Doing the dishes
Doing some shopping for things we need	Cleaning or straightening up a bit
Doing the laundry	Mending my partner's clothes
Doing an errand	Mowing the lawn
Taking out the garbage	Setting the alarm clock
Feeding or taking care of the pets	Having an enjoyable conversation
Telling my partner something confidential	Making some extra money
Starting a conversation with my partner	Summarizing my partner's point of view
Asking my partner how he/she feels	so she/he knows I am listening
Doing something my partner asked	Forgiving my partner for something
Helping to dress the children	Asking for my partner's opinion
Giving my partner a nice greeting when	Smiling at my partner or laughing with
we meet after being apart	him/her
Giving my partner a massage or rub down	Initiating sex
Talking to my partner when he/she	Hire a video
asks for some attention	Being nice to my partner's friends
Trying to cheer my partner up	Paying my partner a compliment
Touching my partner affectionately	Being nice to my partner even though
Looking nice (dress, shaving, etc.)	he/she was mean
Hugging or kissing my partner	Praising my partner
Making his/her favorite food	Responding to sexual advances
Cuddling	Bringing my partner a present
Doing something sexual he/she really likes	Showing that sex was enjoyable
Talking together about finances to help	Shopping for something together
us stick to the budget	Talking about his/her friends or relatives
Going out to dinner, movie or a tavern	Talking together about making a purchase
Playing sports together	Spending time together having fun
Playing games together	Planning or helping with a social event
Suggesting something fun for us to do	Doing something together in the evening

Discussing Intimate Details About Sexuality Can Be Uncomfortable for Some Educators

Some educators do not feel comfortable discussing sex explicitly with couples, and this can impair their capacity to deliver Couple CARE for Parents effectively. Ultimately practice helps a great deal to increase comfort and confidence in running all units of Couple CARE for Parents, and that is true for the sexuality unit as well. Here are some useful strategies to increase personal comfort of the educator. First, start saying sexually explicit words out loud in private, and read through some of the suggested educator statements listed in this book out loud. Talk with a colleague about running the sexuality unit, and explain to them some of the key ideas and concepts to be covered. Ask the colleague to pose questions of you that couples might ask and practice your answers. (For example, ask the colleague to take the role of a man who asks you "*Is it normal for her to never feel like sex?*" or the role of a woman who asks "*Intercourse is uncomfortable, I feel very dry. Is that normal?*") Sit in on a session run by a colleague who feels comfortable with the sexuality unit. Then run the sexuality unit jointly with that colleague. (The colleague can be introduced as the sex expert to the couple.)

Discussing Intimate Details About Sexuality Can Be Uncomfortable for Some Partners/Couples

Some partners/couples do not wish to discuss any of the sexual intimacy activities, e.g., their response to each invitation is "*We are doing fine*" or "*We don't want to talk about this section of the course.*" The educator has an important role in providing a model of open, comfortable discussion about sexuality. However, sex is private for many people. The educator needs to respect each partners' and each couples' level of comfort in discussing sexuality. This unit explores some aspects of sexuality in detail, but couples are not required to talk about these details with their educator. As noted in Chap. 1, the Couple CARE for Parents program is based on adult learning principles in which the partners select what they wish to focus upon to enhance their relationship and adjustment to parenthood. Therefore, the unit can be completed successfully by couples without them having to share responses with the educator.

Partner/Couple Discloses Sexual Dysfunction

Some partners disclose significant sexual dysfunction when doing this unit. It can be helpful to explore briefly the nature of that dysfunction. In the event that those problems are longstanding then providing referral for more intensive assistance might be most helpful. On the other hand, if the dysfunction has started during pregnancy or after the birth, then the dysfunction might be due to complications arising from childbirth or from being new parents. The most common sexual dysfunctions in men are low sexual desire, premature ejaculation, and erectile difficulties. The most common sexual dysfunctions in women are low sexual desire and anorgasmia. Table 7.10 sets out some common ways in which parenthood affects sexual dysfunction and how to address those issues. This can be a useful handout to review with couples.

Painful intercourse is also a common sexual dysfunction, and has some distinctive risk factors in women who have recently given birth. Pain needs to be distinguished

Table 7.10 Common sexual dysfunctions affected by new parenthood

Dysfunction	Possible contribution of parenthood	Ideas worth trying
Male and female loss of sexual desire	Fatigue Reduced couple time Changes in woman's body—hormones Unhelpful sexual self-talk by either partner Stress Male perceives his partner as less sexually attractive (swollen breasts, stretch marks, surgical scar)	Seek more support to get more rest. Increase caring for each other, do couple activities, do romantic things, sensual massage. Challenge unhelpful self-talk. Practice stress management techniques Increase sexual allure—Wear attractive night clothes in silky or sheer materials; shower before bed to be softly scented and fresh
Male premature ejaculation	Reduced frequency of sex speeds up ejaculation	Masturbation to reduce sexual tension, take sex slowly; try to have sex more often with the goal of slowing ejaculation
Male impotence	Fatigue, stress	Seek more support to get more rest; increase healthy lifestyle (gentle exercise, eat well, do not drink too much, do not smoke)
Female anorgasmia	Fatigue, stress, hormonal changes	Seek more support to get more rest; increase healthy lifestyle; do couple activities, do romantic things, sensual massage

from discomfort. As noted earlier most women experience some discomfort during the first few attempts at intercourse after the birth. Discomfort that occurs mainly around the labia (vaginal lips) often can be relieved by use of lubricants. However, if there is severe or deep seated pain, then the woman should be referred for medical assessment. Birth can sometimes cause injuries that lead to sexual pain, which might require treatment.

Chapter 8
Looking Ahead

Chapter Highlights

- The educator helps couples identify likely life changes and plan how to manage those changes.
- The educator reviews with couples early warning signs of relationship deterioration, and how to respond constructively to get their relationship back on track.
- The educator reviews with couples what they will do to sustain their relationship together.

The final unit of Couple CARE for Parents is focused on maintaining relationship satisfaction long term. The unit begins with a review of the content and self-change plan of the previous unit on caring and sexuality. The new content in this unit addresses three areas. First, couples identify changes likely to occur in their lives over the next year or two, discuss the possible positive and negative relationship effects of those life changes, and develop a plan to enhance the positive effects of life changes. Second, the couple is encouraged to consider what might be the early warning signs of relationship problems, and what they could do to prevent the development of serious relationship problems. Third, the couple is encouraged to maintain an ongoing focus on their relationship by developing rituals to celebrate their relationship, and developing strategies for continuing to practice their most important relationship enhancing habits.

Electronic Supplementary Material: The online version of this chapter (doi:10.1007/978-1-4939-1613-9_8) contains supplementary material, which is available to authorized users.

W.K. Halford et al., *Clinical Guide to Helping New Parents*,
Springer Series on Couples and Health, DOI 10.1007/978-1-4939-1613-9_8

Reviewing the Intimacy and Sexual Self-Change Plan

Even couples with good sex lives find the active discussion that Unit 5 encourages can be helpful. The following review is of a husband who had set a self-change goal of talking to his wife about their sex life together since the baby arrived. It illustrates how a husband learned more about his wife's sexual interests, and how they had been influenced by becoming a parent.

Educator: "What stands out in your mind, Gerard as the most important part of last week's unit?"

Gerard: "I had been avoiding talking about sex with Susie. She just does not seem keen since the baby, and I was … was not wanting to pressure her. My worry is that the few times we had sex she just went along to please me, she really didn't seem into it. It surprised me that she said having sex a bit more would be good."

Educator: "Susie, what is your take on this?"

Suzie: "I enjoy sex, or at least I really did before the baby. In the first few months I was so tired. Frankly sex was the last thing I thought about. Gerard is right in that I did sort of just go along when we first started having sex. But now I .. I would like a bit more, you know… (giggles)."

Educator: "A bit hard to talk about with me here?"

Suzie: "It is, but there is something else too .. I feel less sexy you know? My tummy is floppy, my boobs are different. I told Gerard I felt funny about whether or not I still interested him. I've been thinking more about sex, missing the closeness."

Educator: "So having a baby has changed your appearance some, and you feel unsure if Gerard still finds you sexy? But you would like sex more often?"

Suzie: "It sounds like a kid on her second date, right? Does he still like me? But yeah I have an appetite, but I do avoid looking in the mirror."

Gerard: "When we spoke this week, I just said 'Do I find you sexy? Hell yeah', (Laughs) I've only be holding back cause I thought you weren't interested."

Educator: "Right, so talking made you both realize that Suzie was keen to have sex, at least some of the time, but she was worried you were less interested in her. And you were holding back because you worried she was not interested. And what effect do you think knowing that might have?"

Gerard: "I know what effect it had on Thursday morning." (laughs).

Educator: "Right" (smiles). "Suzie: what, if anything, would you like to say to Gerard about the effects of having the discussion together about sex?"

Suzie: "Our sex life has been good. I think me approaching Gerard sometimes, like Thursday, sometimes will be good for both of us. Next week I just might look for a chance to initiate, if Gerard behaves himself. I quite liked surprising him."

Of course not every self-change plan goes exactly as intended. Aaron's self-change plan outcome described below illustrates how there is usually some useful learning to be had even when plans go slightly awry.

Educator: "Aaron, how did the self-change plan go?"

Aaron: "Not quite as planned. I had this idea of like a really romantic evening. The baby was settled, I had cooked a nice meal – a curry, some wine, candles on the dinner table, soft music. I even bought some scented massage oil. I had thought it all out."

Educator: "Sounding good so far. Melissa?"

Melissa: "Almost all of the planning was really good. The curry was hot, I mean really hot."

Educator: "So what happened?"

Aaron: "Melissa was a sport, she tried to eat it. I like my curries hot, but man it even stopped me. She has this easily upset gut and felt pretty dreadful. Long story short, didn't need the massage oil. She and I slept badly, then the baby woke early, and we both felt ragged."

Educator: "So Aaron you went to a lot of trouble, by the sound of it. What was good about what you did?"

Aaron: "Not much really. Melissa has a cold, probably from missing out on sleep."

Educator: (gentle laughter) "He really tried so hard didn't he Melissa?"

Melissa: (Laughing) "Yeah he did. My smooth lover had it all beautifully planned, and now I am coughing and sneezing so bad he's on the couch trying to get some sleep."

Educator: "So Melissa what did you like about Aaron's plan?"

Melissa: "It was the effort, that was the good thing. When we first met he was so romantic, but we've got busy and somehow…" (dabbing her eye with a tissue). "I miss being… like… romanced."

Aaron: "Babe, you know I love you. Maybe I'll try again, but no curry."

Educator: "So, Aaron it seems that even though the evening was not as you planned, it meant a lot to Melissa that you went to the effort and tried a romantic evening."

This passage illustrates a very important theme that occurs in many couples' experience of doing Couple CARE for Parents. When people experience their partner genuinely making an effort to be loving, to be romantic, to be considerate, to listen more effectively, it makes them feel loved, it draws the two partners closer together. Imperfect effort is a world away from no effort at all.

Managing Change

All couples will experience a range of changes during a lifetime together. Many of these changes require the couple to adapt their relationship to changed life circumstances. All the couples doing Couple CARE for Parents have just become parents, which is in itself a huge change. Further changes are likely as their child grows, perhaps as another baby comes along, parents change their paid work and child care arrangements, and so it goes.

Helping couples to manage the relationship effects of life change involves three steps. First, couples reflect on the common changes in couples' lives, and the possible relationship effects of those changes. Second, the couple identifies life changes

Table 8.1 Likely changes in our life together

Change	In 2 years?	In 10 years?
A partner returning to paid work after a break		
A partner changing to work more paid hours		
A partner changing to a different job		
More responsibility at work		
Change home within same city/area		
Change home to a new city/area		
A partner finishing a course or other training		
A partner starting a course or other training		
Birth of another child		
A relative needing special care		
Major purchase (e.g., home or business)		
A major change in social activities		
A major change in sporting activities		
A major change in artistic activities		
Other:		
Other:		

that are likely to occur for them in the next year or two, and the relationship effects of those changes. Finally, the couple is asked to develop a plan to maximize the positive gains, and reduce the negative effects, of those anticipated life changes.

The educator should introduce this activity at the end of Unit 5, saying something like the following "*In the last unit of Couple CARE for Parents you will be identifying one or two major life changes you might experience in the next year or two, the positive and negative effects of those changes and how you can plan to manage the effects these changes might have on your relationship. There are some good examples of common life changes for new parents listed in Table* 8.1 *and Table* 8.2 *is an illustration of how a couple might work through the three steps.*"

Clinical Connection
What have been the most important changes in your life situation in the last 5 years? What positive and negative impacts have those changes had on your closest relationship? How might your experiences be used constructively in sessions you run with couples?

"*In the Table* 8.2 *example, Zi Huang and partner John are discussing Zi Huang's return to part-time work after giving birth to their first child. You see how the couple first identifies the direct effects of the change. For example, the new job means more money and more hours committed to work, and having to work different times of day. Then the couple listed the possible impact of these changes on their, which included less time together, and a* rebalancing *of work and family commitments.*

Table 8.2 Example of planning for change
Change: *Zi Huang is returning to work half time next month*

1. Direct effects of change	2. Possible effects on our relationship	3. Our plan to deal with relationship effects
1. *Zi Huang will have less time to attend to cleaning and cooking*	1. *If Zi Huang kept doing all her current chores plus work she might feel resentful. John may find it hard to get used to doing more of the chores*	1. *We need to develop new routines for getting chores done. We need to agree on who does what. We need to talk this one through*
2. *We'll have more money*	2. *We'll be able to save or spend money differently*	2. *We could spend our money in lots of ways* (e.g., *save for a mortgage, get a cleaner to help with chores). We need to agree on our priorities and agree on a budget. Organize for cleaners to come in each week*
3. *Zi Huang will probably be more tired than now, she may need time to adjust to the demands of her new job*	3. *Zi Huang might feel the need for support from John*	3. *John will take care to have regular couple time to talk to Zi Huang*
4. *We will both be busier*	4. *Having less time to talk may result in us being more stressed with each other*	4. *Both of us to remember that this is a time of change and may be stressful at first. We need to have a regular date to have fun*
5. *We both are unsure how the baby will adjust to day care*	5. *If we are stressed about how little Nan is finding day care, we might be irritable with each other*	5. *We should visit the day care place again. Maybe have Nan do a few half days to get her used to the place, and see how we manage*

Table 8.3 Planning for change handout

Planning for change
Change (1): ....

1. Direct effects of change	2. Possible effects on our relationship	3. Our plan to deal with relationship effects

Finally, the couple listed a plan to deal with the relationship effects of the change. Does the activity make sense?" (Table 8.3).

During the phone or video-conference debrief the educator's aim is to assist couples have realistic and helpful plans for managing future change together effectively. The dialog below provides an example of how an educator helped Michael and Carol.

Educator: "What change did you identify as possibly occurring in the next year or two?"

Michael: "We chose to explore the effects of us swapping role. I am planning a year as a full time Dad. Carol stopped work a few years back, but next year she will go out and be the bread winner."

Educator: "Full time parenting, that does sound exciting. Michael, what did you list as the positive effects of that change?"

Michael: "The reduction in pressure, I am a bit over my job to be honest. Having fun with Dan."

Educator: "Wonderful, wonderful. And what did you list as challenges in this change?"

Michael: "None at all. No work stress, wondering what else I might do with my spare time in the couple of days he is in day care. Golf maybe?"

Educator: "So it feels like it's all upside, with no possible challenges?"

Michael: "None that I can think of."

Educator: "Carol, what did you list as the positive and negative effects of this change?"

Carol: "Well I love the idea of Mike having more time with Danny, that's a positive effect, but I am not sure about day care for a couple of days - I think I see day care as a negative effect. Also, I have been out of the work force for a while and I never earned as much as Mike. I worry we will be short of money, so I listed possible money concerns as a negative effect. Also, looking after a child does take a lot of time. I am not sure Mike quite gets yet how much time it will take him so I listed another possible negative effect that Mike might find parenting stressful, overwhelming."

Educator: "So Carol you listed three challenges, and you both listed Mike's opportunity to be with Dan as a positive. You want to realize your longtime dream of sharing parenthood. But it sounds like, for Carol at least, you need to be confident you have enough money to get by, you need to feel Mike understands what he is getting into – the demands of parenthood, and finally, you need to decide if you will use day care?" (Mike and Carol nod.) "Mike, what was it like to hear Carol list these three concerns about this change?"

Mike: "Actually, I had been sort of thinking about the money one myself too – and the cost of day care, will we manage? But, I really want to spend more time with Dan – he's growing up so fast."

Educator: "Uh huh… It's important for you to have a chance to spend more time with Dan, and Carol agrees this is important. You both also agree that your change might lead to money worries. What did you write down as possible effects of this change on your relationship?"

Carol: "I wrote that we would be closer because we would both understand and can talk about the day to day of parenting – Mike would learn more of what it is like and that shared conversation would be really great. I also, thought, though that the money worries might make us tense with each other- maybe we would argue more about what to spend money on – like day care?"

Educator: "Yes, those are to important possible relationship outcomes. Mike what did you have down?"

Mike: (pause)…"Nothing actually…I couldn't think of any relationship effects at the time. What Carol says is good though – I agree those things could happen to us."

The above discussion illustrates how a brief coaching intervention, in this case prompting the couple to talk through positive and negatives about a future change led the couple to openly talking through the challenges in their plan for Michael to spend more time being a father, both in terms of the direct effects of the change and the effects on their relationship. In reviewing this process with Michael and Carol, Michael commented that he had avoided talking about money and the cost of day care for Daniel because he was concerned that considering these issues might prevent the arrangement of him leaving work from happening. The planning activity with the coaching from the educator led the couple to discuss these concerns further resulting in one of the options to manage the effects being for Michael to consider a change of job and a move to part-time work.

Practice Tip
When reviewing attempts to manage change, prompt the person to examine both positive and negative potential effects of the anticipated change. Someone conducting a thorough review of the likely effect of changes helps that person to develop better management plans.

In reviewing management of change it is important to recognize that flexibility is often needed. Couples with a new baby often find their plans have to be modified. For example, Maggie and Brian had a 6-month-old son, Sean. The couple had discussed adjusting to parenting a baby together. The educator reviewed the discussion with the couple as follows.

Educator: "What's the issue you two were discussing?"
Maggie: "How hard it is to be parents in your late 30s. When I was expecting Amelia I planned to take a week or two maternity leave and then back to work. I love my work. But I had a 30 hour labor, and in the end needed a cesarean."
Brian: "Poor Maggie was wiped out; she got a post-operative infection, and had to go back into hospital. Amelia still doesn't sleep through the night."
Educator: "It sounds like a much tougher journey than you anticipated."
Brian: "Oh yeah. So we're wondering how to get back in control."
Educator: "What options did you come up with?"
Maggie: "Well Brian reckons we should ask the hospital if they ever take babies back." (Laughs.). "Look we would never give little Milly back, but some days it feels like we're drowning."
Educator: "Having a young baby can be truly exhausting. I remember when my kids were really young, and our son had been sick. My wife and I had got no sleep for a couple of nights. I stumbled into the bathroom in the middle of the night and my wife was showering with a tracksuit on. The poor woman was so tired she had no idea what she was doing. About that time we asked her Mum to help us out for a few weeks. I am wondering what you have thought about?"

Practice in Focus
As educators gather more experience working with couples, you can share the wisdom you have gained about how different couples manage the challenges of parenthood. At the same time it is important to recognize a key component of giving good suggestions: timing. The educator has first to listen to the views of each partner, understand what the couple has already considered, and only then should a suggestion be offered.

Maggie and Brian were initially somewhat stuck with generating other options. But they recognized that they were not coping, and something needed to change. Maggie was working half-time, and was reluctant to cut back work any further. Eventually they resolved that Brian would ask his work to let him take some half-time leave, so he could give Maggie more time off from parenting. The best option for any couple varies according to their circumstances, but those who plan ahead tend to manage stressful life changes more effectively than those couples who do not plan. At the same time it is important for the educator to draw out the need for couples to modify their plans when the unexpected comes along.

Preventing Couple Relationship Problems

Sometimes couple relationships go wrong. The focus in Couple CARE for Parents is working with currently satisfied couples to help them sustain high relationship satisfaction. However, problems might develop in the future. It is important to assist the partners to think about early warning signs that a relationship is developing problems, and to do things early to prevent problems.

There are a couple of issues related to discussing potential future problems. First, many couples have unrealistically optimistic views of their future relationship satisfaction, particularly in the early stages of a relationship. One study found that over 90 % of recently married couples report that there is zero or close to zero probability that they will ever separate from their spouse (Fowers, Lyons, & Montel, 1996). Yet, we know that upwards of half of all marrying couples do divorce. The rates of breakup are even higher in cohabiting couples.

Clearly many couples have unrealistic illusions that there are guaranteed positive relationship outcomes. Often this romantic unreality is conveyed by comments like, "she is my soul mate, we will always love each other," and, "from the moment we met I knew he was the one." Couples with such positive illusions are sometimes resistant to considering the possibility that their relationship might encounter difficulties in the future. Due to this potential resistance to considering future relationship problems, the topic of how to manage emerging problems is not explicitly dealt with in Couple CARE for Parents until toward the end of the program. This is intended to allow the major focus of the program to be on relationship enrichment during this major life transition, and leave addressing the potentially sensitive issue of preventing couple problems to when hopefully, the relationship between the educator and each couple is strong.

There are a few points worth making about the nature of couple relationship problems, and the risk of separation. The educator can summarize these briefly saying something like the following:

"About 40% of married couples and about 60% of cohabiting couples separate. Doing Couple CARE for Parents is a really important step you have taken to strengthen your relationship, which reduces your risk of developing relationship problems. Another thing you can do is understand what leads to separations, how you can detect early warning signs of a deteriorating relationship, and what to do about it."

"About half of all separations result from serious relationship problems. Violence, severe chronic arguments that get nasty, mental health problems like depression or alcohol abuse, and affairs. In Couple CARE for Parents we emphasize the idea of self-change, of each person taking responsibility for strengthening the relationship. But there are some behaviors that a partner might do that are unacceptable to you, but which you have little influence over. For example, when men are severely violent toward their female partner it seems to have little or nothing to do with her behavior. Rather, those men often have persistent long-established patterns of violence toward others. A woman who finds herself the victim of such violence might have few options within the relationship to alter the man's behavior. Similarly, if your partner has a severe drinking or gambling problem, that could wreck things for both of you. If you have tried to get someone to change a real problem like that, and they refuse... Well, that is what divorce is for. Getting out of a bad relationship is a good idea."

"However, half of divorces happen in couples that do not have high conflict, or obvious severe problems. It seems more like the relationship has lost its spark. When asked about why they divorced, these people say things like, "We just sort of grew apart. We stopped communicating. The magic had faded". Now wanting a good relationship seems pretty reasonable. But divorcing someone because the relationship is a little jaded is a bit like finding your car is low on petrol and abandoning it at the side of the road. The car needs fuel, not to be abandoned."

The Unit 6 handout included as Table 8.4 asks partners to identify early warning signs of relationship deterioration and how they might deal with these. The debrief-

Practice Tip

It is important to help couples distinguish between intolerable behaviors and potentially acceptable behaviors. Intolerable behaviors include things no one should have to experience, like violence or heavy drug or alcohol use. At the same time, no partner is ever like to do everything exactly as one might want and acceptance of the spouse's shortcoming is needed for sustaining a relationship. Some examples of behaviors that can be annoying, but potentially are acceptable, are not always pulling their weight with certain chores, not expressing themselves clearly, and not expressing affection quite as you might like.

Table 8.4 Early warning signs handout

Early warning sign	What I might do
Example: My partner and I are arguing a bit more than usual. This goes on for months	1. Revisit the program materials, refresh our conflict management skills 2. Look into relationship therapy

talking about a difficult issue on more than one occasion; (c) finding you tend to do the same things over and over, and that the fun is not really there; (d) the frequency of expressing love or caring has dropped away; (e) you have an argument and bad feelings persist; (f) you or your partner drop away from doing your fair share of the parenting or household chores; or (g) your interest or enjoyment of sex had declined.

Clinical Connection
This list of warning signs might look familiar to the couples, as it summarizes failing to do some of the key things promoted in Couple CARE for Parents. What other warning signs might be useful to draw to couples' attention?

There are three issues that are useful to highlight after discussing early warning signs of a deteriorating relationship. First, problems often develop over a period of time. Second, addressing problems is most effective when it is done early in the development of the problem. Paying attention to the relationship and working to keep it strong is a vital investment in having a good life together. Third, talk with your partner about any issues that worry you and try to find things you personally can change to make things better. If the relationship does not improve from your own efforts, go for help and go early. Couple therapy is very effective when couples go with smaller problems that have recently developed. A couple tune-up is a very good investment. Couple therapy when there are long-standing and severe problems is worth a try, but it is less effective than going early.

It is important to conclude the review of prevention of relationship problems on a positive note. I often make the transition to a final review of the Couple CARE for Parents program with the following along the following lines:

"*We have focused on potential problems because we know problems can occur. If problems develop and you cannot resolve them yourself, then seeking help early gives you a good shot to turn things around. By being attentive to your relationship, using the skills you have learned through Couple CARE for Parents, you can reduce the chance that such problems will occur. So let's turn to maintaining a relationship focus and continuing to apply what we have covered in Couple CARE for Parents.*"

Relationship Maintenance

An introduction to the importance of relationship maintenance might go something like the following: "*Sustaining a relationship through the ups and downs of a long life together is not always easy. Nobody is kind, attentive, supportive and effective at communication all the time. What makes a real difference is putting in some effort from time to time. Perfect relationships do not exist. But truly wonderful relationships do. You have been working to make your relationship as good as you can, and the final activity or Couple CARE for Parents asked you to consider how you can sustain your relationship across the years.*"

Celebrating the Couple Relationship

Most couples develop rituals in which they celebrate their relationship together. Some couples have regular rituals such as a cup of tea together on a weekend morning, or a drink together early in the evening. There also might be less frequent rituals like a romantic dinner for their wedding anniversary, or a celebration of each other's birthdays.

The idea of relationship rituals can be introduced by describing the idea in similar terms to those in the preceding paragraph. During the telephone or videoconference the educator can ask questions such as "*How do you currently celebrate your relationship? What did you list as the two new things you could each do in the future to celebrate your relationship?*" to explore when, where and how the couple currently celebrate their relationship, and what they plan to do in the future to keep celebrating their relationship. If the couple struggles to come up with ideas for celebrating their relationship the educator could ask them what they see other couples, family or friends doing. Or, if the couple is really struggling, the educator can offer the ideas listed in Table 8.5 and send it to the couple after the session.

Maintaining Use of Relationship Skills

After each unit of Couple CARE for Parents each partner is asked to reflect on what ideas they most liked from that unit, and to identify how they might apply the ideas they liked. The last exercise of the Couple CARE for Parents program is an attempt to draw together the learning from across the program, and help partners to identify what relationship skills they believe are most important for them to sustain. Table 8.6 lists the key relationship skills covered in the Couple CARE for Parents program. The educator can ask each person to rate the extent to which they feel they understand and could demonstrate that skill if asked. If a partner cannot remember a skill,

Table 8.5 Couple relationship celebration rituals

Together assemble and look through photographs of important relationship events (e.g., holidays, birthdays, anniversaries, family gatherings)
Make a photo album about your child's life to date
A weekend at home together when you don't see anyone else, and do fun things together that are different to what you usually do
An in-home date (e.g., picnic in the back yard) where you make a special effort to do something that will be fun for your partner
Cook a special meal for your partner
Have a glass of wine or cup of tea together and catching up on the day's happenings
Plan fun time together, such as a holiday or special outing
Work on a fun project together (e.g., build something for your child)
Plan a special meal to celebrate a birthday or anniversary
Get out the diary and booking in a special couple activity
Get together with family to celebrate your relationship
Send a card to your partner telling them how you feel about them
Do a community service activity together

or misunderstands the skills then the educator can review the skill with the couple on the phone during the debriefing.

The educator should then ask each participant to identify three skills from Couple CARE for Parents that they want to keep doing. Some couples find it useful to specify a date and plan to review with their partner how they are maintaining key skills they recorded as useful to them. Most couples seem to prefer less structure, but still find the checklist useful to prompt their memory of what to include in their maintenance planning.

The educator might also ask some of the following questions: "*What is the most important thing you have learnt from doing Couple CARE for Parents? What is one thing you want to continue to do to enhance your couple relationship?*" A core message for participants is that the Couple CARE for Parents is just one more step in their relationship together. What matters is that the partners each take responsibility for nurturing and sustaining their relationship. For example, if the couple has a disagreement, this can cue one or both partners to review how they manage differences, and to develop a self-change plan to help them manage conflict more effectively. Similarly, if either partner is feeling the need to express more caring, or be more supportive of their partner, then they can develop a self-change plan to address that identified relationship need.

We usually conclude the final session by asking the couple "*Are there any other questions or comments either of you have about what we have covered across the whole program?*" Finally, we suggest that the handouts provided are a useful resource of the couple, particularly the checklist summarizing the skills covered in the program. We encourage the couple to refer back to this list from time to time to generate ideas on how they can continue to enhance their relationship.

Table 8.6 Key skills covered in couple care for parents

Skills	Do I know?	Important?	My pick(s)
Parenting			
Shared and realistic expectations about infant care			
Realistic shared expectations of parenting			
Identify and address support needs			
Communication			
Describe specifics			
Express positives			
Assert negatives clearly and politely			
Self-disclose feelings			
Pay attention			
Show you are listening			
Summarize content			
Paraphrase feelings			
Ask questions			
Hear your partner out			
Give feedback constructively			
Stress management			
Describe specifics			
Express preferences			
Conflict resolution			
Describe specifics			
Caring and sex			
Prompt self-reflection and partner feedback on expressions of caring			
Express preferences			
Challenge unhelpful self-talk about sexuality			
Balance responsibility for initiating			
Looking ahead			
Plan for change			
Monitor for early warning signs, discuss any issues			
Respond to early warning signs of problems			
Celebrate the relationship			

Some Final Comments

The couple has now completed their final session. Hopefully at this point each partner has a broad understanding of the diverse influences on their relationship, and a shared vision of the sort of relationship they want together. This knowledge, combined with the capacity to work effectively on their relationship with self-change, empowers each partner to nurture their relationship. When a couple completes relationship education neither they nor we can know the long-term fate of their relationship. Relationship education is only one influence on their relationship future. The couple may face severe future stresses that undermine their relationship. If that is the case, then hopefully our program better prepares them to recognize early the warning signs of problems, and that they take steps to improve the relationship. Couples often find that the effort each extends to succor their relationship, and their collective ability to support each other, enriches their individual and shared fates.

As professionals we, the authors, have seen the support and joy partners feel when their relationship goes well, and also have seen and felt the suffering of clients and friends when relationships come to painful ends. When our time as professionals with a couple comes to an end, we hope that this couple will experience the joy of truly loving, and being loved by, their partner. The work you do as a health professional, and as a couple relationship educator, is an important contribution toward helping more couples achieve lasting, loving relationships. Thank you for the service you provide to couples. We hope the ideas in this book will assist you in this important work.

References

Abdool, Z., Thakar, R., & Sultan, A. H. (2009). Postpartum female sexual function: A review. *European Journal of Obstetrics, Gynecology, and Reproductive Biology, 145*(2), 133–137. doi:10.1016/j.ejogrb.2009.04.014.

American Academy of Pediatrics. (2012). Breastfeeding and the use of human milk. *Pediatrics, 129*(3), 600–603. doi:10.1542/peds. 2011-3553.

Astone, N. M., Dariotis, J. K., Sonenstein, F., Pleck, J., & Hynes, K. (2010). Men's work effort and the transition to fatherhood. *Journal of Family and Economic Issues, 31*(1), 3–13. doi:10.1007/s10834-009-9174-7.

Australian Bureau of Statistics. (2012). *Australian social trends*. Canberra, Australia: Australian Government Publisher.

Barnard, K. E. (2010). Keys to developing early parent–child relationships. In K. E. Barnard & J. D. Sparrow (Eds.), *Nurturing children and families: Building on the legacy of T. Berry Brazelton* (pp. 53–63). New York: Wiley-Blackwell. doi:10.1002/9781444324617.ch5.

Belsky, J., & Kelly, J. (1994). *Transition to parenthood: How a first child changes a marriage: Why some couples grow closer and others apart*. New York: Delacorte Press.

Blyth, R., Creedy, D. K., Dennis, C. L., Moyle, W., Pratt, J., & De Vries, S. M. (2002). Effect of maternal confidence on breastfeeding duration: An application of breastfeeding self-efficacy theory. *Birth, 29*(4), 278–284. doi:10.1046/j.1523-536X.2002.00202.x.

Bodenmann, G., & Cina, A. (2006). Stress and coping among stable-satisfied, stable-distressed and separated/divorced Swiss couples: A 5-year prospective longitudinal study. *Journal of Divorce & Remarriage, 44*(1–2), 71–89. doi:10.1300/J087v44n01_04.

Bouchard, G., Boudreau, J., & Hebert, R. (2006). Transition to parenthood and conjugal life comparisons between planned and unplanned pregnancies. *Journal of Family Issues, 27*(11), 1512–1531. doi:10.1177/0192513X06290855.

Bradbury, T. N., & Fincham, F. D. (1987). Affect and cognition in close relationships: Towards an integrative model. *Cognition and Emotion, 1*(1), 59–87. doi:10.1080/02699938708408364.

Bradbury, T. N., & Karney, B. R. (2004). Understanding and altering the longitudinal course of marriage. *Journal of Marriage and Family, 66*(4), 862–879. doi:10.1111/j.0022-2445.2004.00059.x.

Clark, A., Skouteris, H., Wertheim, E. H., Paxton, S. J., & Milgrom, J. (2009). My baby body: A qualitative insight into women's body-related experiences and mood during pregnancy and the postpartum. *Journal of Reproductive and Infant Psychology, 27*(4), 330–345. doi:10.1080/02646830903190904.

Claxton, A., & Perry-Jenkins, M. (2008). No fun anymore: Leisure and marital quality across the transition to parenthood. *Journal of Marriage and Family, 70*(1), 28–43. doi:10.1111/j.1741-3737.2007.00459.x.

W.K. Halford et al., *Clinical Guide to Helping New Parents*,
Springer Series on Couples and Health, DOI 10.1007/978-1-4939-1613-9

Copen, C. E., Daniels, K., Vespa, J., & Mosher, W. D. (2012). *First marriages in the United States: Data from the 2006–2010 National Survey of Family Growth* (National Health Statistics Reports No. 49). Hyattsville, MD: National Center for Health Statistics.

Cowan, C. C., & Cowan, P. (1992). *When partners become parents: The big life change for couples*. Mahway, NJ: Lawrence Erlbaum Associates.

Cowan, P. A., Cowan, C. P., Pruett, M. K., Pruett, K., & Wong, J. J. (2009). Promoting fathers' engagement with children: Preventive interventions for low-income families. *Journal of Marriage and Family, 71*(3), 663–679. doi:10.1111/j.1741-3737.2009.00625.x.

Cox, J. L., Holden, J. M., & Sagovsky, R. (1987). Detection of postnatal depression: Development of the 10-item Edinburgh Postnatal Depression Scale. *British Journal of Psychiatry, 150*, 782–786.

Craig, L., & Bittman, M. (2005). *The effect of children on adult's time use: An analysis of the incremental time costs of children in Australia*. Australia: Social Policy Research Centre.

Crockenberg, S. C., Leerkes, E. M., & Lekka, S. K. (2007). Pathways from marital aggression to infant emotion regulation: The development of withdrawal in infancy. *Infant Behavior & Development, 30*(1), 97–113. doi:10.1016/j.infbeh.2006.11.009.

Doss, B. D., Rhoades, G. K., Stanley, S. M., & Markman, H. J. (2009). The effect of the transition to parenthood on relationship quality: An 8-year prospective study. *Journal of Personality and Social Psychology, 96*(3), 601. doi:10.1037/a0013969.

Dyrenforth, P. S., Kahsy, D. A., Donnellan, M. B., & Lucas, R. E. (2010). Predicting relationship and life satisfaction from personality in nationally representative samples from three countries: The relative importance of actor, partner and similarity effects. *Journal of Personality and Social Psychology, 99*(4), 690–702. doi:10.1037/a0020385.

Elliston, D., McHale, J., Talbot, J., Parmley, M., & Kuersten-Hogan, R. (2008). Withdrawal from coparenting interactions during early infancy. *Family Process, 47*, 481–499. doi:10.1111/j.1545-5300.2008.00267.x.

Erel, O., & Burman, B. (1995). Interrelatedness of marital relations and parent–child relations: A meta-analytic review. *Psychological Bulletin, 118*(1), 108.

Evanoo, G. (2007). Infant crying: A clinical conundrum. *Journal of Pediatric Health Care, 21*(5), 333–338.

Feeney, J., Hohaus, L., Noller, P., & Alexander, R. (2001). *Becoming parents: Exploring the bonds between mothers, fathers and their children*. New York, NY: Cambridge University Press.

Florsheim, P., Sumida, E., McCann, C., Winstanley, M., Fukui, R., Seefeldt, T., & Moore, D. (2003). The transition to parenthood among young African American and Latino couples: Relational predictors of risk for parental dysfunction. *Journal of Family Psychology, 17*(1), 65. doi:10.1037/0893-3200.17.1.65.

Fowers, B. J., Lyons, E. M., & Montel, K. H. (1996). Positive marital illusions: Self-enhancement or relationship enhancement? *Journal of Family Psychology, 10*, 192–208. doi: 10.1037/0893-3200.10.2.192.

France, K. G., Blampied, N. M., & Hnederson, J. M. T. (2003). Infant sleep disturbance. *Current Pediatrics, 13*, 241–2546. doi:10.1016/S)957-5839(03)0004-6.

Galland, B. C., Taylor, B. J., Elder, D. E., & Herbison, P. (2012). Normal sleep patterns in infants and children: A systematic review of observational studies. *Sleep Medicine Reviews, 16*(3), 213–222. doi:10.1016/j.smrv.2011.06.001.

Gettler, L. T., & McKenna, J. J. (2011). Evolutionary perspectives on mother–infant sleep proximity and breastfeeding in a laboratory setting. *American Journal of Physical Anthropology, 144*(3), 454–462. doi:10.1002/ajpa.21426.

Glenn, N. D. (1998). The course of marital success and failure in five American 10-year cohorts. *Journal of Marriage and the Family, 60*, 269–282. doi:10.2307/353529.

Goddard, H. W., Marshall, J. P., Olson, J. R., & Dennis, S. A. (2012). Character strengths and religiosity as predictors of marital satisfaction in a sample of highly religious and divorce-prone couples. *Journal of Couple & Relationship Therapy, 11*(1), 2–15. doi:10.1080/15332691.2011.613308.

Gottman, J. M., & Notarius, C. I. (2000). Decade review: Observing marital interaction. *Journal of Marriage and Family, 62*(4), 927–947. doi:10.1111/j.1741-3737.2000.00927.x.
Halford, W. K. (2001). *Brief couple therapy*. New York: Guilford.
Halford, W. K. (2011). *Marriage and relationship education: What works and how to provide it*. New York: Guilford Press.
Halford, W. K., Lizzio, A., Wilson, K. L., & Occhipinti, S. (2007). Does working at your marriage help? Couple relationship self-regulation and satisfaction in the first 4 years of marriage. *Journal of Family Psychology, 21*(2), 185–194. doi:10.1037/0893-3200.21.2.185.
Halford, W. K., & Petch, J. (2010). Couple psychoeducation for new parents: Observed and potential effects on parenting. *Clinical Child and Family Psychology Review, 13*, 164–180. doi: 10.1007/s10567-010-0066-z.
Halford, W. K., Petch, J., & Creedy, D. K. (2010). Promoting a positive transition to parenthood: A randomized clinical trial of couple relationship education. *Prevention Science, 11*(1), 89–100. doi:10.1007/s11121-009-0152-y.
Halford, W. K., Sanders, M. R., & Behrens, B. C. (2000). Repeating the errors of our parents? Family-of-origin spouse violence and observed conflict management in engaged couples. *Family Process, 39*, 219–235. doi:10.1111/j.1545-5300.2000.39206.x.
Halford, W. K., Sanders, M. R., & Behrens, B. C. (2001). Can skills training prevent relationship problems in at-risk couples? Four-year effects of a behavioral relationship education program. *Journal of Family Psychology, 15*(4), 750. doi:10.1037/0893-3200.15.4.750.
Hansson, M., & Ahlborg, T. (2012). Quality of the intimate and sexual relationship in first-time parents—A longitudinal study. *Sexual & Reproductive Healthcare, 3*(1), 21–29. doi:10.1016/j.srhc.2011.10.002.
Henderson, J. M. T., France, K. G., & Blampied, N. M. (2011). The consolidation of infants' nocturnal sleep across the first year of life. *Sleep Medicine Reviews, 15*, 211–220. doi:10.1016/j.smrv.2010.08.003.
Henderson, J. M. T., France, K. G., Owens, J. L., & Blampied, N. M. (2010). Sleeping through the night: The consolidation of self-regulated sleep across the first year of life. *Pediatrics, 126*(5), 1081–1087.
Hewitt, B., & De Vaus, D. (2012). Change in the association between premarital cohabitation and separation Australia 1945–2000. *Journal of Marriage and the Family, 71*(2), 353–361.
Hipp, L. E., Kane Low, L., & van Anders, S. M. (2012). Exploring women's postpartum sexuality: Social, psychological, relational, and birth-related contextual factors. *The Journal of Sexual Medicine, 9*(9), 2330–2341. doi:10.1111/j.1743-6109.2012.02804.x.
Holman, T. (2001). *Premarital prediction of marital quality or breakup: Research, theory, and practice*. New York, NY: Springer.
Houts, R. M., Barnett-Walker, K. C., Paley, B., & Cox, M. J. (2008). Patterns of couple interaction during the transition to parenthood. *Personal Relationships, 15*(1), 103–122. doi:10.1111/j.1475-6811.2007.00187.x.
Iafrate, R., Bertoni, A., Margola, D., Cigoli, V., & Acitelli, L. K. (2012). The link between perceptual congruence and couple relationship satisfaction in dyadic coping. *European Psychologist, 17*(1), 73. doi:10.1027/1016-9040/a000069.
Johnson, C. E. (2011). Sexual health during pregnancy and the postpartum. *Journal of Sexual Medicine, 8*(5), 1267–1284. doi:10.1111/j.1743-6109.2011.02223.x.
Katz-Wise, S. L., Priess, H. A., & Hyde, J. S. (2010). Gender-role attitudes and behavior across the transition to parenthood. *Developmental Psychology, 46*(1), 18. doi:10.1037/a0017820.
Kazantzis, N., Deane, F. P., Ronan, K. R., & L'Abate, L. (Eds.). (2005). *Using homework in cognitive behavioral therapy*. New York: Routledge.
Klemetti, R., Kurinczuk, J. J., & Redshaw, M. (2011). Older women's pregnancy related symptoms, health and use of antenatal services. *European Journal of Obstetrics, Gynecology, and Reproductive Biology, 154*(2), 157–162. doi:10.1016/j.ejogrb.2010.10.025.
Kolb, D. A. (1984). *Experiential learning: Experience as the source of learning and development* (Vol. 1). Englewood Cliffs, NJ: Prentice-Hall.

Krishnakumar, A., & Buehler, C. (2000). Inter-parental conflict and parenting behaviours: A meta-analytic review. *Family Relations, 49*(1), 25–44. doi:10.1111/j.1741-3729.2000.00025.x.

Larson, J. H., & Holman, T. B. (1994). Premarital predictors of marital quality and stability. *Family Relations, 43*(2), 228–237. doi:10.2307/585327.

Lizzio, A., & Wilson, K. (2004). Action learning in higher education: An investigation of its potential to develop professional capability. *Studies in Higher Education, 29*(4), 469–488. doi:10.1080/0307507042000236371.

Manikam, R., & Perman, J. A. (2000). Pediatric feeding disorders. *Journal of Clinical Gastroenterology, 30*(1), 34–46. doi:10.1097/00004836-200001000-00007.

Meijer, A. M., & van den Wittenboer, G. L. (2007). Contribution of infants' sleep and crying to marital relationship of first-time parent couples in the 1st year after childbirth. *Journal of Family Psychology, 21*(1), 49. doi:10.1037/0893-3200.21.1.49.

Mitnick, D. M. H., Richard, E., & Smith Slep, A. M. (2009). Changes in relationship satisfaction across the transition to parenthood: A meta-analysis. *Journal of Family Psychology, 23*(6), 848–852. doi:10.1037/a0017004.

Neff, L. A., & Karney, B. R. (2004). How does context affect intimate relationships? Linking external stress and cognitive processes within marriage. *Personality and Social Psychology Bulletin, 30*(2), 134–148. doi:10.1177/0146167203255984.

O'Brien, M., & Peyton, V. (2002). Parenting attitudes and marital intimacy: A longitudinal analysis. *Journal of Family Psychology, 16*(2), 118. doi:10.1037/0893-3200.16.2.118.

Owen, M. T., & Cox, M. J. (1997). Marital conflict and the development of infant–parent attachment relationships. *Journal of Family Psychology, 11*(2), 152. doi:10.1037/0893-3200.11.2.152.

Perini, T., Ditzen, B., Hengartner, M., & Ehlert, U. (2012). Sensation seeking in fathers: The impact on testosterone and paternal investment. *Hormones and Behavior, 61*(2), 191–195. doi:10.1016/j.yhbeh.2011.12.004.

Perren, S., Von Wyl, A., Bürgin, D., Simoni, H., & Von Klitzing, K. (2005). Depressive symptoms and psychosocial stress across the transition to parenthood: Associations with parental psychopathology and child difficulty. *Journal of Psychosomatic Obstetrics & Gynecology, 26*(3), 173–183. doi:10.1080/01674820400028407.

Petch, J. F., Halford, W. K., Creedy, D. K., & Gamble, J. (2012). A randomized controlled trial of a couple relationship and coparenting program (Couple CARE for Parents) for high- and low-risk new parents. *Journal of Consulting and Clinical Psychology, 80*(4), 662–673. doi:10.1037/a0028781.

Pinquart, M., & Teubert, D. (2010). Effects of parenting education with expectant and new parents: A meta-analysis. *Journal of Family Psychology, 24*(3), 316–327. doi:10.1037/a0019691.

Pope, S., Evans, S., McLean, N., & Michael, C. (1998). *Psychosocial adjustment and postnatal depression in mothers and fathers in the year following delivery* (pp. 35–37). Women & Infants Research Foundation Western Australia Annual Report 1997.

Rhoades, G. K., Stanley, S. M., & Markman, H. J. (2012). A longitudinal investigation of commitment dynamics in cohabiting relationships. *Journal of Family Issues, 33*(3), 369–390. doi:10.1177/0192513x11420940.

Rourke, L., & Anderson, T. (2002). Using web-based, group communication systems to support case study learning at a distance. *International Review of Research in Open and Distance Learning, 3*(2), 1–13.

Sadeh, A. (1996). Stress, trauma, and sleep in children. *Child and Adolescent Psychiatric Clinics of North America, 5*, 685–700. doi:10.1037/0012-1649.36.3.291.

Sagiv-Reiss, D. M., Birnbaum, G. E., & Safir, M. P. (2012). Changes in sexual experiences and relationship quality during pregnancy. *Archives of Sexual Behavior, 41*(5), 1241–1251. doi:10.1007/s10508-011-9839-9.

Sanders, M., Halford, W., & Behrens, B. (1999). Parental divorce and communication in engaged couples. *Journal of Family Psychology, 14*, 60–78. doi:10.1037/0893-3200.13.1.60.

Schulz, M. S., Cowan, C. P., & Cowan, P. A. (2006). Promoting healthy beginnings: A randomized controlled trial of a preventive intervention to preserve marital quality during the transition to

parenthood. *Journal of Consulting and Clinical Psychology, 74*, 20–31. doi:10.1037/0022-006X.74.1.20.
Schwalb, M. E., Schwald, B. J., & Lamb, M. (2013). Final thoughts: Comparisons and conclusions. In M. E. Schwalb, B. J. Schwald, & M. E. Lamb (Eds.), *Fathers in cultural context* (pp. 312–345). New York: Routledge.
Shapiro, A. F., & Gottman, J. M. (2005). Effects on marriage of a psycho-communicative-educational intervention with couples undergoing the transition to parenthood, evaluation at 1-year post intervention. *The Journal of Family Communication, 5*(1), 1–24. doi:10.1207/s15327698jfc0501_1.
Sinai, D., & Tikotzky, L. (2012). Infant sleep, parental sleep and parenting stress in families of mothers on maternity leave and in families of working mothers. *Infant Behavior & Development, 44*(6), 1314–1325. doi:10.1016/j.paid.2007.11.024.
Smith, L., Heaven, P. C., & Ciarrochi, J. (2008). Trait emotional intelligence, conflict communication patterns, and relationship satisfaction. *Personality and Individual Differences, 44*(6), 1314–1325.
Stanley, S. M. (2001). Making the case for premarital education. Family Relations, 50, 272–280. doi:10.1111/j.1741-3729.2001.00272.x.
Story, L. B., & Bradbury, T. N. (2004). Understanding marriage and stress: Essential questions and challenges. *Clinical Psychology Review, 23*(8), 1139–1162. doi:10.1016/j.cpr.2003.10.002.
Story, L. B., Karney, B. R., Lawrence, E., & Bradbury, T. N. (2004). Interpersonal mediators in the intergenerational transmission of marital dysfunction. *Journal of Family Psychology, 18*(3), 519. doi:10.1037/0893-3200.18.3.519.
Teixeira, C., Figueredo, B., Conde, A., Pacheco, A., & Costa, R. (2009). Anxiety and depression during pregnancy in women and men. *Journal of Anxiety Disorders, 11*, 142–148. doi:10.1016/j.jad.2009.03.005.
Teng, A., Bartle, A., Sadeh, A., & Mindell, J. (2012). Infant and toddler sleep in Australia and New Zealand. *Journal of Paediatrics and Child Health, 48*(3), 268–273. doi:10.1111/j.1440-1754.2011.02251.x.
Tharner, A., Luijk, M. P., Raat, H., IJzendoorn, M. H., Bakermans-Kranenburg, M. J., Moll, H. A., & Tiemeier, H. (2012). Breastfeeding and its relation to maternal sensitivity and infant attachment. *Journal of Developmental & Behavioral Pediatrics, 33*(5), 396–404. doi:10.1097/DBP.0b013e318257fac3.
Thomas, A., & Sawhill, I. V. (2005). For love and money? The impact of family structure on family income. *The Future of Children, 15*(2), 57–74. doi:10.1353/foc.2005.0020.
Trillingsgaard, T., Baucom, K. J., Heyman, R. E., & Elklit, A. (2012). Relationship interventions during the transition to parenthood: Issues of timing and efficacy. *Family Relations, 61*(5), 770–783. doi:10.1111/j.1741-3729.2012.00730.x.
Twenge, J. M., Campbell, W. K., & Foster, C. A. (2003). Parenthood and marital satisfaction: A meta-analytic review. *Journal of Marriage and Family, 65*(3), 574–583. doi:10.1111/j.1741-3737.2003.00574.x.
Vanzetti, N. E., & Duck, S. E. (1996). *A lifetime of relationships*. Belmont: Thomson Brooks/Cole Publishing Co.
Weston, R., Qu, L., & Hayes, A. (2012). From form to function: Contemporary choices, changes and challenges. In P. Noller & G. Karantzas (Eds.), *Couples and family relationships: A guide to contemporary research, theory, practice and policy* (pp. 1–42). Hoboken, NJ: Wiley-Blackwell.
Whisman, M. A. (2007). Marital distress and DSM-IV psychiatric disorders in a population-based national survey. *Journal of Abnormal Psychology, 116*, 638–643.
Wicki, W. (1999). The impact of family resources and satisfaction with division of labour on coping and worries after the birth of the first child. *International Journal of Behavioral Development, 23*(2), 431–456. doi:10.1080/016502599383900.
Wilson, K. L., & Halford, W. K. (2008). Processes of change in the flexible delivery of couple relationship education. *Family Relations, 57*, 625–635. doi:10.1111/j.1741-3729.2008.00529.x.

Wood, R. G., McConnell, S. D., Moore, Q., Clarkwest, A., & Hsueh, J. (2012). The effects of building strong families: A healthy marriage and relationship skills education program for unmarried parents. *Journal of Policy Analysis and Management, 31*(2), 228–252. doi:10.1002/pam.21608.

Wood, R. G., Moore, Q., Clarkwest, A., Killewald, A., & Monahan, S. (2012). *The long-term effects of building strong families: A relationship skills education program for unmarried parents*. Washington, DC: Office of Planning, Research and Evaluation, Administration for Children and Families, U.S. Department of Health and Human Services (OPRE).

Wurmser, H., & Papousek, M. (2008). Facts and figures: Database of the Munich interdisciplinary research and intervention program for fussy babies. In M. Papousek, M. Schieche, & H. Wurmser (Eds.), *Disorders of behavioral and emotional regulation in the first years of life* (pp. 27–52). Washington, DC: Zero to Three Press.

MIX
Papier aus verantwortungsvollen Quellen
Paper from responsible sources
FSC® C105338

If you have any concerns about our products,
you can contact us on
ProductSafety@springernature.com

In case Publisher is established outside the EU,
the EU authorized representative is:
Springer Nature Customer Service Center GmbH
Europaplatz 3, 69115 Heidelberg, Germany

Printed by Libri Plureos GmbH
in Hamburg, Germany